FRANCE IN FOCUS: IMMIGRATION POLICIES, FOREIGN POLICY AND U.S. RELATIONS

J. B. LYNCH
EDITOR

Novinka Books
An imprint of Nova Science Publishers, Inc.
New York

Copyright © 2006 by Novinka Books
An imprint of Nova Science Publishers, Inc.

For permission to use material from this book please contact us:
Telephone 631-231-7269; Fax 631-231-8175
Web Site: http://www.novapublishers.com

NOTICE TO THE READER

The Publisher has taken reasonable care in the preparation of this book, but makes no expressed or implied warranty of any kind and assumes no responsibility for any errors or omissions. No liability is assumed for incidental or consequential damages in connection with or arising out of information contained in this book. The Publisher shall not be liable for any special, consequential, or exemplary damages resulting, in whole or in part, from the readers' use of, or reliance upon, this material.

This publication is designed to provide accurate and authoritative information with regard to the subject matter covered herein. It is sold with the clear understanding that the Publisher is not engaged in rendering legal or any other professional services. If legal or any other expert assistance is required, the services of a competent person should be sought. FROM A DECLARATION OF PARTICIPANTS JOINTLY ADOPTED BY A COMMITTEE OF THE AMERICAN BAR ASSOCIATION AND A COMMITTEE OF PUBLISHERS.

Library of Congress Cataloging-in-Publication Data:
Available Upon Request

ISBN: 1-59454-935-4

Published by Nova Science Publishers, Inc. ✤
New York

RANCE IN FOCUS: IMMIGRATION POLICIES, FOREIGN POLICY AND U.S. RELATIONS

CONTENTS

PREFACE

France has taken its own course for centuries and it continues to do so. Its immigration policies have now led to very widespread and very public burnings of automobiles and rioting. Its millions of Arab citizens with their high birth rates, high unemployment rates, and high frustration levels have reached the level of ignition. Can France put this situation back into the bottle or can it change its policies in time to prevent a constant level of civil unrest? This book examines those policies themselves as well as France's foreign policies which are intertwined with the problems.

In: France in Focus   ISBN 1-59454-935-4
Editor: J.B. Lynch, pp. 1-10   © 2006 Nova Science Publishers, Inc.

Chapter 1

IMMIGRATION IN FRANCE[*]

Emmanuel Peignard

Immigration is not just one of today's sensitive political issues, it also offers an opportunity to examine social ties, national integration and citizenship.

REASONS FOR MIGRATION

France is a traditional country of immigration: for over 150 years, while other countries have been combining high birth rates and emigration, France has been taking in foreign populations to prevent her demographic decline. Even today, immigration is still in some cases put forward as the remedy for the ageing of the national population.

Arch defender of human rights, France also likes to think of herself as a land of asylum for political refugees. Since the beginning of the last century she has taken in, inter alia, Italians, Poles, White Russians, Ukrainians, Armenians, Spanish Republicans, Chileans and Asians. In 1952, France signed the 1951 Geneva Convention which governs current asylum methods and created the Office français de protection des réfugiés et apatrides (OFPRA - French Office for the Protection of Refugees and Stateless Persons).

---

[*] Excerpted from http://www.ambafrance-us.org/atoz/immigration.asp

In France, an industrializing country, manpower requirements led to the twentieth century's two main waves of immigrants: to rebuild the country after the First World War in the 1920s and for the same reasons in the 1960s (1956 to 1973). The Office national d'immigration (ONI – National Immigration Office) was set up in 1946 to organize the recruitment of the foreign workers required to meet the needs of the boom in industry.

Lastly, family reunification is the final main reason for migration. At the outset, immigrant workers were not supposed to settle in France; as single people, they were allocated to hostels. Over the years, however, immigrants increasingly began to arrive with their families – or arranged for them to come over. Other forms of accommodation were then needed. Some (such as temporary hostels) were to remain squalid places.

In July 1974, when economic growth was slowing down, the government announced that immigration would officially be brought to an end, although the right to asylum and family reunification would continue. The latter then became the main source of immigration: it predominates in the statistics of the ONI, which in 1987 became the Office des migrations internationales (OMI – International Migration Office).

FOREIGNERS AND IMMIGRANTS: THE FIGURES

A distinction needs to be drawn between foreigners and immigrants. The former are simply people who do not have French nationality. The latter are people living in France who were born abroad. Consequently, not all foreigners are immigrants and, in particular, immigrants who have acquired French nationality are no longer foreigners. Nowadays, over one third of immigrants (36%) have become French. These facts must be borne in mind when looking at statistics on foreigners in France.

The 1999 general population census shows a 9% fall in the number of foreigners since 1990, for two main reasons: naturalizations (550,000 during the period) and deaths (190,000). In March 1999, 3,260,000 foreigners were resident in metropolitan France (i.e. 5.6% of the population).

The number of immigrants is, however, stagnating, as it has increased in much the same way as the total population over the last ten years (3.4%): 4,310,000 immigrants were resident in France in March 1999.

NATIONAL ORIGINS OF IMMIGRANTS

Immigration to France was initially from other European countries: Italy, Belgium and Poland up to the Second World War and then Spain and in particular Portugal after the war. In the 1950s, immigration from Africa – the Maghreb to start with, and then sub-Saharan Africa – increased in absolute and relative terms. More recently, countries of origin have diversified with a rise in Asian nationals (especially from south-east Asia: +35% between the two censuses) and, to a lesser extent, Turks (+16%) and immigrants from eastern Europe. The main increase, however, has been among the population from sub-Saharan Africa which tripled between 1982 and 1990 and has almost doubled (+43%) in the last ten years.

Between 1962 and 1975, Italians were the largest immigrant population (32%) ahead of Spaniards, Poles and Algerians. Since 1975, Portuguese people have been the largest community of foreign origin, with Algerians the second largest. Their numbers are smaller, however, than those of north Africans as a whole (Algerians + Moroccans + Tunisians).

According to INSEE (National Institute of Statistics and Information about the Economy), the geographical origins of foreigners became more diversified between 1990 and 1999: people of European origin totalled only 1,600,000, i.e. a decline of 9.3% in comparison with 1990. This decline has been continuous for over 25 years: European nationals accounted for 57% of the foreign population in 1975, 49% in 1990 and 45% in 1999.

More often than not, migratory flows initially involve single workers and then families. Consequently, to begin with, the immigrants' age structure differs from that of the overall population: more male and adult. Subsequently, permanent family reunification leads to their population pyramid becoming like that for the French as a whole: the male immigrant population is ageing (22% fewer foreigners aged under 30 in 1999 than in 1990, while the over-40s increased by 15%). The number of men and women is also tending to level out.

POSITION OF IMMIGRANTS: DISPARATE DATA

Statistics on foreigners and immigrants are tricky to draw up: differentiating between French people on the basis of their parents' national origin may lead to risks of discrimination (the use of the register of Jews by the Vichy Regime in the Second World War is a tragic example of this). This is why only foreigners, i.e. people permanently resident in France who state that they do not have French nationality, are officially registered. Immigrants are not registered as such once they have become French: they disappear as immigrants from the general population census. Moreover, unlike most of the other EU member States, France has no municipal population register to which everyone, whether foreign or not, must report their arrival in the commune [smallest administrative subdivision in France].

Statistical data are dispersed between different government departments, and serve different purposes:

- INSEE (National Institute of Statistics and Information about the Economy] conducts the population census;
- OMI (the International Migration Office) registers arrivals;
- the Population and Migration Directorate records the number of naturalizations;
- OFPRA (French Office for the Protection of Refugees and Stateless Persons) deals with asylum applications;
- the Ministry of the Interior issues residence permits;
- the Ministry of Justice is responsible for acquisitions of nationality;
- and INED (National Institute for Demographic Research) presents to Parliament an annual report on the demographic situation.

These data use different terminology and figures and analyse different variants. It is therefore difficult to use them to draw up statistics on immigrants.

INTEGRATION OF IMMIGRANTS: POLITICAL FRAMEWORK

Immigrants always remain attached to their community of origin and their national or "ethnic" culture. Nevertheless, their participation in civic, community and economic life is also shaped by the political traditions of host societies. Some countries have relied on immigration for their development (United States, Canada, Australia, Argentina, etc.) while others have tended during their history to avoid immigration (the European countries in general). This is one of the reasons why the integration model of a nation-State cannot be transposed.

There are three main models of integration for foreigners and immigrants:

- The so-called German ethnic model according to which nationality is conferred chiefly by descent (jus sanguinis), language, culture and religion; foreign "ethnic" groups are regarded as being impossible to assimilate and the policy does not therefore aim to transform them into nationals;
- The so-called French "political" model, according to which nationality together with citizenship is based largely on acceptance of the droit du sol, which is a combination of residence and jus soli [place of birth] and in which "ethnic" identities are confined to private life rather than spilling over into the public sphere (secularism); the implicit aim is the individual integration of each immigrant by schools and other institutions;
- The British/US model in which minorities are recognized (in community life, but not legally) as political players; here, ideological differences may lead to collective forms of segregation: ethnic neighbourhoods, and segregation in social activities and in the workplace.

ACQUIRING FRENCH NATIONALITY

The rules on nationality are set out in the basic order of 19 October 1945 (amended in 1973, 1984, 1993 and 1998). They are based on the jus soli (droit du sol) – people are French because of their place of birth and residence (France) even if their parents are foreign – and on the jus sanguinis (droit du sang [blood right]) – people are French whatever their place of birth and residence provided that their parents are French.

The three main ways in which French nationality can be gained are:

- naturalization, i.e. the granting of nationality to people who have reached their majority (18 years) and have lived in France for at least five years;
- acquisition, in the case of 18-year-old children of foreigners born in France and resident there for at least five years between the ages of 11 and 18 (under Article 44). Although between 1993 (Act of 22 July) and 1998 (Act of 16 March) applicants had to "manifest a

desire" to become French in order to enjoy this right, this is no longer required.

• declaration, following marriage to a French man or woman (the marriage must have lasted at least one year).

PUBLIC INTEGRATION POLICIES

According to the Republican tradition, public policies cannot take account of nationality of origin; measures discriminating positively in favour either of foreign immigrants or of French people are not admissible. Foreigners enjoy civil, social and economic rights on a par with those of national citizens; political rights (the right to vote and be elected) are confined to the latter. For instance, systems and measures to combat unemployment and promote occupational integration cannot be aimed at immigrants as a specific population, but may target them as "disadvantaged" groups, like the long-term unemployed, single parents, the disabled and young people with no qualifications.

However, the task of the FAS (Social action fund for immigrant workers and their families - Fonds d'action sociale pour les travailleurs immigrés et leurs familles), set up in 1958, is to foster the social integration of immigrants through measures for families, children and young people in the areas of housing (participation in the management of migrant workers' hostels), training (including literacy) and employment.

ACHIEVEMENTS OF THE FRENCH POLICY TO INTEGRATE FOREIGNERS

Generally speaking, observers agree that the French integration model has been successful: the earlier waves of immigration (from Italy, Poland, Belgium, Spain, etc.) have been assimilated; the more recent ones (from Portugal and the Maghreb) appear to be being integrated socially, culturally and politically – although their economic and occupational integration is not yet complete. Reference to standard integration criteria seems to bear this out:

• nationalization statistics confirm the model's efficacy: when immigrants' children had to "manifest" the desire to be French, when applying for French nationality, the overwhelming majority did so; they now acquire it automatically;

- there are many mixed marriages (between French people and foreigners): according to the 1999 census, 9.6% of the 271,361 marriages celebrated in 1998 were with a foreign spouse;
- at school, according to sociologists, in comparable socio-economic and family circumstances, immigrants' children are at least as successful as other young French people;
- as regards housing, there are not strictly speaking any ghettoes; "problem" districts contain vulnerable people from a variety of different backgrounds. It should nevertheless be borne in mind that close on two thirds of immigrants live in towns of more than 200,000 inhabitants (one third live in Ile de France).

Nevertheless, in some areas the French integration model seems to be running out of steam, although the causes of the problems faced by immigrants tend to be socio-economic (working class backgrounds, few vocational qualifications) rather than "ethnic" (foreign backgrounds, national cultures):

- schooling: young foreigners are less likely than others to follow a "normal" school career (collège [mixed-ability school for children aged between 11 and 15 approximately], general education lycée [catering for children between 15 and 18 years of age] and then higher education). French middle-class families also use various strategies to avoid sending their children to schools with a high percentage of foreign children (dispensations from school catchment areas, enrolment in private education, etc.). Schools may themselves be "elite" establishments or, on the contrary, de facto, "ethnic" ones catering for a homogenous group of disadvantaged pupils.
- housing: the most socially and economically disadvantaged, among whom immigrants are over-represented, tend to be concentrated in certain districts, estates, or high-density housing complexes;
- employment: in 1995, there were 1.97 million (7.8% of France's total active population) active foreigners (i.e. those in or looking for jobs). 46% of these were manual workers (compared with an average of only 26% for the country as a whole). Immigrants tend, moreover, to be working class whatever their country of origin – with particularly high levels among Moroccans and Algerians. The

immigrant population has much lower job security (fixed-term contracts, temporary work). They also suffer badly from unemployment (20% of active foreigners were unemployed in 1995 in comparison with a national average of 12%). Non-European nationals are the worst affected: in March 1998 their unemployment rate, based on the International Labour Office (ILO) standard, was 31.4% in comparison with 11% for French people. Young foreigners (aged 15 to 24) are in an even more difficult position: their unemployment rate rose from 22% to 43% between 1992 and 1996, while the rate for young French people increased only from 16.2% to 21% over the same period.

The causes of these integration problems are not only economic and social (lack of education and qualifications, few financial resources, social problems, etc.), but also have to do with mutual cultural perceptions.

- Discrimination against immigrants is seen particularly when they are looking for jobs. Openly discriminatory job offers are illegal, but many other, more discreet practices escape the clutches of the law. Consequently, the number of legal convictions (74 in 1995 and 81 in 1996) does not show the whole picture.
- Racism is targeted in particular against peoples whose presence evokes a conflict-ridden colonial past: immigrants from the Maghreb are the main targets of hostility (more so than other Africans and far more so than Asians, and particularly the Portuguese). Support for Islam, which many people consider impossible to integrate into French civilization or at the very least to be incapable of embracing a secular culture, but which is nevertheless France's second religion, is perceived in the worst of cases as a challenge to the national tradition of integration. This feeling of foreignness is fuelled by differences in customs (women's status, lifestyles, family authority, etc.).

Looking at this from a historical perspective, it is important to remember that all groups of immigrants, whatever their original nationality, religion, skin colour or customs, have been victims of racism. Xenophobia is often linked to periods of economic depression and the notions of "tolerance threshold" or "inability to integrate" are devoid of any sociological meaning.

PROSPECTS FOR THE INTEGRATION
OF IMMIGRANTS IN FRANCE

Nowadays, immigration into France has to be seen in a European context; on the one hand, because the integration paths of European and non-European immigrants are diverging (better integration of the former because they are EU citizens; emergence of the notion of "European racism" working against the latter) and, on the other, because national immigration and integration policies are now in line with the Community Treaties which set out the frameworks for action by member States. Moreover, member States are now being confronted by the same problems: radical economic changes, employment crisis, urban segregation, marginalization of unskilled workers, calling into question of education systems, racism, etc.).

Each country has its own way of integrating its population depending on its political tradition. At the same time, however, asylum and immigration policy is becoming a Community matter: under the Schengen Agreements (1985 and 1990), the signatory countries had already agreed, for instance, to harmonize conditions for the issue of short-stay visas. The Treaty of Amsterdam (Article 73k), signed in 1997, states that the Council of the Union should draw up measures in two areas of immigration policy: entry and residence conditions (issue of visas and long-term residence permits, including for the purpose of family reunion, by the member States) and illegal immigration and illegal residence. In the long term, these decisions will be taken by qualified majority. EU nation-States will nevertheless retain the right to decide independently how to form themselves into communities of citizens.

ACKNOWLEDGEMENTS

Emmanuel Peignard is a sociologist and researcher at the Université de Bourgogne. The opinions given in this article are solely those of the author.

BIBLIOGRAPHY

Dewitte, Philippe (ed.), *Immigration et intégration. L'état des savoirs*, La Découverte, 1999

Haut Conseil à l'Intégration, *L'intégration à la française, Report to the Prime Minister,* La Documentation française, 1993

Noiriel, Gérard, *Le creuset français,* Seuil, 1988

Schnapper, Dominique, *L'Europe des immigrés. Essai sur les politiques d'immigration,* François Bourin, 1992

Todd, Emmanuel, *Le destin des immigrés. Assimilation et ségrégation dans les démocraties modernes,* Seuil, 1994

Tribalat, Michèle, *Faire France. Une enquête sur les immigrés et leurs enfants,* La Documentation française, 1995.

Embassy of France in the United States - May 2001

In: France in Focus   ISBN 1-59454-935-4
Editor: J.B. Lynch, pp. 11-49   © 2006 Nova Science Publishers, Inc.

Chapter 2

FRANCE: FACTORS SHAPING FOREIGN POLICY, AND ISSUES IN U.S.-FRENCH RELATIONS[*]

Paul Gallis

SUMMARY

The factors that shape French foreign policy have changed since the end of the Cold War. The perspectives of France and the United States have diverged in some cases. More core interests remain similar. Both countries' governments have embraced the opportunity to build stability in Europe through an expanded European Union and NATO. Each has recognized that terrorism and the proliferation of weapons of mass destruction are the most important threats to their security today.

Several factors shape French foreign policy. France has a self-identity that calls for efforts to spread French values and views, many rooted in democracy and human rights. France prefers to engage international issues in a multilateral framework, above all through the European Union. European efforts to form an EU security policy potentially independent of NATO emerged in this context.

From the September 11, 2001, attacks on the United States through the Iraq war of 2003 until today, France has pressed the United States to confront emerging crises within a multilateral framework. France normally wishes to "legitimize" actions ranging from economic sanctions to political censure to military action in the United Nations. Bush Administration officials have at times reacted with hostility to such efforts, charging that French efforts to ensure "multipolarity" in the world are a euphemism for organizing opposition to U.S. initiatives. Trade and investment ties between the United States and France are extensive, and provide each government a large stake in the vitality and openness of their respective economies. Through trade in goods and services, and, most importantly, through foreign direct investment, the economies of France and the United States have become increasingly integrated.

Other areas of complementarity include the Balkans peace operations, the stabilization of Afghanistan, and the fight against terrorism — all challenges where France has played a central role. A major split occurred over Iraq, however, with many countries either supporting or independently sharing French ideas of greater international involvement.

Developments in the Middle East affect French foreign and domestic policy. France has a long history of involvement in the region, and a population of 5-6 million Muslims. Paris believes that resolution of the Arab-Israeli conflict is key to bringing peace to the region, and that the United States too strongly favors the Israeli government, a U.S. tendency that impedes peace, in the French view. Surges in violence in the Middle East have led to anti-Semitic acts in France, mostly undertaken by young Muslims.

This report will be updated as needed. See also its companion report, CRS Report RL32459, *U.S.-French Commercial Ties*, by Raymond J. Ahearn.

This report was written at the request of the co-chairs of the Congressional French Caucus.

INTRODUCTION

The end of the Cold War has altered the U.S.-French relationship. Before the collapse of the Soviet Union, the United States, France, and their NATO allies viewed the USSR as the principal threat to security. France was known for its independent streak in policy-making, both with its European counterparts and the United States, notably under President de Gaulle in the

---

* Excerpted from CRS Report RL32464, dated January 10, 2005.

1960s. Nonetheless, there was cohesion throughout the alliance at such moments as the Berlin crisis of 1961, the Cuban missile crisis the following year, and the debate over basing "Euromissiles" in the 1980s.

Several factors shape French foreign policy. France has a self-identity that calls for efforts to spread French values and views, many rooted in democracy and human rights. France prefers to engage most international issues in a multilateral framework, above all through the European Union (EU). France is also a highly secular society, a characteristic that influences views on the state's relation to religion.

Since the conclusion of the Cold War, the perspectives of France and the United States have diverged in some cases. Most core interests remain similar. Both countries' governments have embraced the opportunity to build stability in Europe through an expanded European Union (EU) and NATO. Each has accepted the need to ensure that Russia remain constructively engaged in European affairs. Each has also recognized that terrorism and the proliferation of weapons of mass destruction are the most important threats today.

Post-Cold War developments have brought new challenges, which have affected the U.S.-French bilateral relationship. German unification and the entry of central European states into the EU and NATO may have shifted the continent's balance of political and economic power away from the French-German "engine" and towards central and eastern Europe. While French-German initiatives remain of great importance in Europe, German perspectives are increasingly eastward; and, in some eyes, central European states feel closer strategically and politically to the United States than they do to France. Nonetheless, France remains a key player in European affairs and few initiatives can succeed without its support and participation.

The United States, a global superpower since the Second World War, has remained deeply involved in European affairs. In the view of some Europeans, however, by the mid-1990s Washington appeared to be slowly disengaging from Europe, while wanting at the same time to maintain leadership on the continent.[1] French and German, and some would say British, efforts to form an EU security policy potentially independent of NATO and the United States emerged and evolved in this period. The Europeans based this policy in part on the belief that the United States had growing priorities beyond Europe, and in part because Americans and Europeans were choosing different means to protect their interests. The U.S. decision to go into Afghanistan in October 2001 with initially minimal allied assistance was one example of this trend; the U.S. war against Iraq, with overt opposition from France and several other allies, was another.

During the Bush Administration, France, with other European allies, has pressed the United States to confront emerging crises within a multilateral framework. Terrorism and proliferation are threats that cross borders, and often involve non-state actors. France, where possible, normally attempts to engage elements of the international community in responding to such threats, and to "legitimize" actions ranging from economic sanctions to political censure to military action at the United Nations. In the view of many U.N. officials, the United States has disparaged the United Nations, and is impatient with its decision-making process.[2] France has promoted a view of a "multipolar" world, with the EU and other institutions representing poles that encourage economic development, political stability, and policies at times at odds with the United States. Bush Administration officials have reacted with hostility to such efforts, charging that "multipolar" is a euphemism for organizing opposition to U.S. initiatives.

Some U.S. observers characterize France as an antagonist. The current French ambassador reportedly has charged that some U.S. officials have deliberately spread "lies and disinformation" about French policies in order to undercut Paris.[3] Occasional mutual antagonism was already evident during the first years of the Fifth Republic (1958-present), when President de Gaulle sometimes offered singular views on international affairs, often at odds with Washington and other allies, and in 1966 withdrew France from the military structures of NATO. In the 1960s, France began to develop its own nuclear deterrent force.

French assertiveness is generally seen in a different, more constructive, light in Europe. Other Europeans often credit French initiatives in the EU and in other institutions as fresh in perspective, or moving a discussion into a new realm; Paris played a major role, for example, in the conception and implementation of the EU's Economic Monetary Union (EMU).

Traditional French assertiveness accounts in some ways for France punching above its weight on the international scene. France is a country of medium size with modest resources. Yet it has played a persistent role, for example, in establishing EMU, building a European Security and Defense Policy (ESDP), and in orchestrating opposition to the U.S.-led Iraq war. While U.S.-French relations have at times been contentious, there is also a complementarity and an intertwining of U.S. and French interests and actions. Nowhere is this more clear than in the realm of commercial interactions.

Trade and investment ties between the countries are extensive, providing each side a big stake in the vitality and openness of their respective economies. Through trade in goods and services, and, most importantly, through foreign direct investment, the economies of France and the United States have become increasingly integrated. Over $1 billion in commercial transactions take place every *business day* of the year between the two sides. This huge amount of business activity, in turn, is responsible for creating an estimated 1.7 million American and French jobs.[4]

Other areas of complementarity include the Balkans peace operations, the stabilization of Afghanistan, and the fight against terrorism — all challenges where France has played a central role. A major split occurred over Iraq, however, with many countries either supporting or independently sharing French ideas of greater international involvement.

This report examines the key factors that shape French foreign policy. From that context, it analyzes some of the reasons for the tensions in and the accomplishments of U.S.-French relations. The report is illustrative, rather than exhaustive. Several important issues, such as the effort to stabilize Haiti and the policy to persuade Iran to open its nuclear program to international inspections, are not examined. Instead, the report reviews other issues selected because they exemplify some of the essential features of the U.S.-French relationship.

FACTORS SHAPING FRENCH POLICY

A Global Perspective

France, like the United States, believes that it has a special role in the world. The core of the perceptions of France's role in the world stems from the Revolution that began in 1789. The Revolution was an event of broad popular involvement: widespread bloodshed, expropriation of property, and execution of the king fed the notion that there could be no turning back to monarchical government. Not only was the monarchy overthrown and a powerful church structure forcibly dismantled, but French armies, and ultimately French administrators in their wake, transformed much of the continent into societies where more representative, democratic institutions and the rule of law could ultimately take root. The Revolution was therefore a central, formative element in modern European history, notably in Europe's evolution from monarchical to democratic institutions. The cultural achievements of France before and since the Revolution have added to French influence. French became the language of the élite in many European countries. By 1900, French political figures of the left and the right shared the opinion that France was and must continue to be a civilizing beacon for the rest of the world.[5]

The view that France has a "civilizing mission" (*la mission civilisatrice*) in the world endures today. For many years, the French government has emphasized the message of human rights and democracy, particularly in the developing world and in central Europe and Eurasia.

Many French officials, particularly Gaullists,[6] have been highly assertive in seeking to spread French values throughout the world. Dominique de Villepin, President Chirac's former foreign minister, has written that "at the heart of our national identity, there is a permanent search for values that might be shared by others." Gaullists have sought to embed French views in EU initiatives, sometimes in concert with Germany and sometimes alone. In 1996, the former Gaullist Prime Minister Alain Juppé called for an "inner circle" in the EU, defined as "a small number of states around France and Germany" that must move forward to secure EMU, a common foreign and security policy, and a military force able to protect the Union's interests. His foreign minister added that such policies, "far from weakening France's influence and authority in the world... will increase their impact and audience."[7] France's rank and influence in the world are important to French policymakers. Membership on the U.N. Security Council, close relations with parts of the Arab world and former worldwide colonies, aspects of power such as nuclear weapons, and evocation of human rights are central to France's self-identity in international affairs.[8]

Others sometimes contest France's evocation of values. By the mid-20th century, some French colonies, such as Algeria and Morocco, sharply disputed whether actual French policy met the ideals of Paris's message. Algeria fought a twenty-year war for independence. Today, some Europeans praise the intellectual underpinnings of French "reason and good sense" that combat "prejudice and fanaticism." However, they see occasional contradictions in French policy, as when France sought to lift sanctions against Iraq when U.N. WMD inspections temporarily ended there in 1998, then only belatedly accepted a new inspections regime in 2002, even though French officials had privately been stating their belief that Iraqi WMD programs were likely continuing, or when France balks at what some view as more democratic power-sharing in the expanding European Union.[9]

The European Union

France was one of the founding members of the European Union (initially known as the European Coal and Steel Community) in 1952. Improved trade and economic development were central objectives of member states in a Europe still struggling from the dislocation caused by the Second World War, but overarching objectives from the beginning were political rapprochement between Germany and its former enemies, and political stability on the continent. The EU was conceived in this context, with strong U.S. support.

France has been a catalyst in achieving greater political unity and economic strength in the European Union. President Chirac has altered the traditional Gaullist view that France could act alone as a global power and be the Union's most important member. Rather, today, the Gaullists believe that France can best exert its power through the EU, acting in tandem with Germany and occasionally with Britain.

Some European governments object to the view that France, Germany, and Britain can guide EU policies. They describe the claim for leadership of the three countries as a nascent "*Directoire*," or initiative to dominate the EU and push smaller member states to follow the three governments' lead. French officials dispute the idea of a "*Directoire*." In their view, initiatives in the Union should not be held back by governments that wish to proceed more slowly. President Chirac describes the efforts of France and Germany, and occasionally Britain, as those of a "pioneer group" that wishes "to go faster and further in European integration." Some French officials say that France "does not wish to be resigned to a Europe which would only be a space of internal peace." Rather, in their view the EU should become a force for positive, broad-reaching change in Europe and the world.[10]

French officials cite a range of examples where a "pioneer group" of EU countries has taken the lead in forging forward-looking policies. France, Germany, and other countries led the way in implementing the Schengen agreement (open borders for people) and EMU, which not all EU countries have embraced. In 2003 and 2004, France, Germany, and Britain played the key role in persuading Iran to accept International Atomic Energy Agency (IAEA) inspections of its nuclear energy sites for possible evidence of nuclear weapons production. French officials state that they want the EU to have a strong Commission and a strong President of the Commission, although the Council, where ministers from member states meet, must remain paramount in decision-making. France has supported initiatives to streamline voting in the EU, and to place more areas of decision-making under "qualified majority voting (QMV)," to avoid a rule under which one government among the 25 member states may veto a decision. For example, France has proposed, unsuccessfully, that foreign-policy decisions be subject to QMV.[11]

French efforts to provide leadership in the EU have occasionally led to contentious disputes with other governments, which sometimes involve the United States. After 15 EU member or candidate states signed two letters in February 2003 backing U.S. policy towards Iraq, President Chirac said that the EU aspirants were "not terribly well-behaved and a little unaware of the dangers that a too rapid alignment with the American position can carry." They lost a good opportunity "to be quiet;" Chirac then appeared to threaten to veto Romania's and Bulgaria's candidacies for membership. Officials from Poland and several other governments that signed the letter sharply criticized Chirac for such comments, and cited the remark as evidence that France wished to dominate the Union and was cool towards EU enlargement. Such instances act to undercut France's leadership in the EU.[12]

Officials in some EU governments believe that France's leadership is constrained by policies occasionally viewed as erratic. In one example, France, with Germany, was a principal progenitor of EMU, conceived to bind the EU economies more closely together by subjecting them to legal strictures over debt and a range of monetary policies. France initially described EMU as above all a political measure, in which EU member states agreed upon joint economic policies for the good of all. When France (and Germany) decided to abrogate the "Stability Pact" governing these policies in late 2003, some member states complained that Paris was acting in its own political interest, at the expense of others.[13] In this view, France had initially persuaded other governments to embrace EMU as a turning point for the Union, but at a moment when its economy was experiencing difficulties decided to walk away from a key element of the policy.

At the same time, Secretary of Defense Rumsfeld's description in 2003 of Europe as divided between "old" (France, and other governments that criticized the Administration's policy towards Iraq) and "new" (those governments that supported Administration policy) has not been well-received in central Europe. While these governments may at times spurn French leadership, and desire a strong strategic partnership with the United States, they nonetheless view EU membership and the continental stability that it may bring as an equally vital interest. These governments believe that they must in the future work closely with France to shape EU political and economic policy, and oppose any Administration efforts to divide the European Union.[14]

Multilateralism

Multilateralism is important to all U.S. allies and in particular to all 25 members of the European Union, which is itself a multilateral entity painfully put together over a fifty-year period. For the Europeans, decision-making in international institutions can lend legitimacy to governmental policies. Member states of the EU share certain attributes of sovereignty and pursue joint policies intended to provide political and economic stability, goals that the United States has supported since the 1950s. Globally, Europeans perceive the United Nations as the locus for decision-making that can provide an international imprimatur for member states' actions in international security. The U.N. carries special significance for European governments that experienced two world wars. Europeans see the EU and the U.N. as belonging to a civilizing evolution towards cooperation rather than confrontation in world affairs.

France is in a key position in the framework of multilateral institutions. It enjoys a permanent seat and holds a veto in the U.N. Security Council. Important EU policies are not possible without French support. French officials play central roles on the European Commission, in the European Central Bank, and the IMF, and are eligible to lead, and have led, each of these institutions.

France wishes to confront the greatest threats to its security through international institutions. The Chirac government identifies terrorism as the country's most important threat. France has considerable experience in combating domestic terrorism and today is generally regarded as highly effective in that domain. At the same time, France believes that an anti-terror foreign policy must include a comprehensive multilateral effort to diminish the prevalence of poverty in the developing world and to encourage the spread of literacy, democracy, and human rights. While military action may also be a tool against terrorism for Paris, French leaders prefer to begin any effort to confront an international threat in a multilateral framework.

The Use of Force and the United Nations

For the French government, the conflict in Iraq in 2003 raised questions about the legitimate use of force. France, together with several other European governments, have been critical of the Bush Administration's national security doctrine that endorses "preemptive action" in the face of imminent danger.

While the French government does not reject the use of force, it maintains that certain criteria must be met for military action to acquire legitimacy. In the words of former Foreign Minister de Villepin, fear of terrorism and other threats make "the use of force is tempting. [Use of force] is justifiable if collective security or a humanitarian crisis requires it. But it should only be a last recourse, when all other solutions are exhausted and the international community, through the Security Council, decides upon the question." President Chirac has stated the same opinion. In a speech to the U.N. General Assembly in clear reference to the U.S. invasion of Iraq, he said, "In today's world, no one can act alone in the name of all and no one can accept the anarchy of a society without rules. There is no alternative to the United Nations.... Multilateralism is essential....It is the [U.N. Security Council] that must set the bounds for the use of force. No one can appropriate the right to use it unilaterally and preventively."[15]

For the most part, France's record over the past decade has been consistent in following the precept that the U.N. must endorse the use of force in a crisis. For example, France, along with other countries, since 1990 has obtained a U.N. resolution for the potential or actual use of force for interventions in the first Gulf War, Bosnia, Afghanistan, Congo, the Ivory Coast, and Haiti. One notable exception came in 1999, when France joined its NATO allies in going to war against Serbia in an effort to prevent ethnic cleansing in Kosovo. In that case, until the eleventh hour, the French government sought a U.N. resolution for NATO's use of force. At the same time, in the face of an increasingly likely Russian veto, French officials and counterparts from several other European allies began indicating that Serbian actions had reached a stage where using force to prevent a humanitarian catastrophe in Kosovo would be justifiable without a U.N. resolution.[16] When a Russian veto became certain, there was a consensus in NATO that the use of force was justifiable in this instance even in the absence of a U.N. resolution.

"Multipolarity"

The Chirac government and the Bush Administration and some of its supporters have clashed over France's pursuit of "multipolarity" in economic, military, and political affairs. The French government has described multipolarity as a system of balance in international affairs, in part a natural outgrowth of trading blocs and regional global differences, in part a value that is in principled opposition to global domination by one power or bloc. Some Administration officials, notably Condoleezza Rice, have disparaged the concept as a means to thwart U.S. foreign policy. In June 2003, she said that it was troubling that "some have spoken admiringly — almost nostalgically — of 'multipolarity,' as if it were a good thing to be desired for its own sake." She said that France seemed intent upon "checking" the United States, and that France appeared to consider "the United States more dangerous than Saddam Hussein."[17] Some Administration supporters in the neoconservative movement are more pointed, and claim that France wishes to reclaim the "*grandeur*" of an earlier era and deny the United States its "unipolar moment"; in this view multipolarity is a concept employed specifically to subvert U.S. foreign policy.[18]

The idea of multipolarity is not new, nor is it French in origin. In recent times, it was a common sentiment in the European Union of the 1990s. It was seen at that time as a means for Europeans, acting together, to put forward their commercial interests in negotiations and reach equitable trade agreements with the United States.[19] French officials have usually tended to describe multipolarity as taking effect across a range of policies. They say that the world is "unipolar" in a military sense, given the U.S.'s overwhelming military power. But they also note that given the proliferation of crises around the globe, the development by the EU of military institutions and units can provide complementary forces in the effort to build order and stability. Chirac has used "multipolarity" in economic terms as well, noting that not only the EU but the rise of China, India, and Mercosur in Latin America have created global commercial competitors. De Villepin contends that "the vision of multipolarity aims in no case to organize rivalry or competition, but rather responsibility, stability, and initiative."[20] As will be discussed below, some U.S. officials believe that French-led EU initiatives are intended to undercut elements of U.S. leadership of NATO.

Religion and the State: "Le Foulard"

France has a long history of religious violence. Political factions went to war in the 16th century over religious differences and dynastic claims; the conflict left many thousands dead and the society badly divided. One cause of the Revolution was a desire by many to end the Catholic Church's grip on elements of society and dismantle a church hierarchy widely viewed as corrupt and poorly educated.

In the late 19th and early 20th centuries, the government sought to ensure that public schools did not become embroiled in religious controversies. Parliament passed a law in 1905 intended to ensure separation between religion and politics. The law enshrined "*laïcité*" as a principle of French life. "Laïcité" is not simply secularism, but rather an attempt to balance religious freedom and public order. The government protects freedom of religion, and there is no state church in France; at the same time, there is an effort to ensure that religious groups do not engage in political activism that would be disruptive of public life.[21]

A current controversy in France has pitted elements of the Muslim community against the government. Approximately 36% of France's Muslim community describe themselves as "practicing."[22] Within this group there are Muslims who seek to ensure that their children may pursue what they view as traditional Islamic practices in France's public school system. Some French Muslim families require their girls to wear head scarves ("le foulard") to school. French public schools are co-educational. Some Muslim families object to elements of co-education; for example, they do not want their female children to take physical education, nor do they want them to take biology classes where reproduction is discussed. Some families also do not want male doctors to treat their female children at public hospitals. The French government believes that such families are causing disruption in the public school system, especially in a period of increased tensions between Muslims and Jews in France, and a period of political tensions with the Muslim world over the issue of terrorism.

After an extended debate, the government presented a bill to Parliament to ban "conspicuous" religious symbols in public schools through the secondary-school level. The law prohibits the wearing of head scarves. It also bans religious symbols such as large crosses and the yarmulke. In the parliamentary debate over the bill, Prime Minister Raffarin said that the purpose of the legislation is "to set limits" in the face of growing religious militancy. Some religious signs "take on a political sense and cannot be considered a religious sign," he said. "I say with force, religion must not be a political subject."[23] Some Muslim governments, such as that of Iran, sharply condemned the bill. Moderate Muslim groups in France supported it as a means to reduce tensions in the school system and in broader society.[24] The bill passed by a wide margin in March 2004, with government parties and elements of the left supporting it.

Some observers in France criticized the bill because they viewed it as essentially a negative instrument. They contend that the government should do more to integrate Muslims into French society. The debate evokes a familiar theme in recent French history. At the turn of the 20th century, for example, many opposed the large migration into France of Italians and Spaniards, ethnic groups viewed as coming from societies where political violence was rife. Yet these groups have become well assimilated into French society, and their members commonly occupy senior positions in politics and the professions. In contrast, many observers in France believe that large elements of the Muslim population have not been assimilated. One observer, a member of the government-appointed commission to study the issue of head scarves in schools, opposed the law. In his view, France should seek a balance that embraces diversity yet preserves a degree of uniformity that sustains the French "identity." He believes that the law fails such a purpose because it stigmatizes the Muslim population.[25]

Anti-Semitism in France

Since 2000, there has been a noticeable increase in anti-Semitic acts of violence in France. Most of the acts have occurred in the suburbs around Paris, and in southern cities such as Marseille and Montpellier. Molotov cocktails have been thrown at several synagogues and schools, rabbis have been assaulted, and in one instance, a school bus with Jewish children was stopped and threatened by a gang of street thugs. No one has been killed in these attacks.[26]

France has a total population of 59.8 million, of whom approximately 600,000 are Jewish. According to a 2002 study by a French Jewish community organization, most French Jews today are white collar professionals, and are well integrated into French society. "Mixed" marriages with non-Jews have become increasingly common in the past two decades, but a strong community sense remains. In a 2002 poll, 42% of the Jewish population said that they keep kosher, while 29% said that they are non-observant. Since the increase in 2000 in anti-Semitic incidents, 6%, mostly young Jews in their 'teens and 'twenties, responded that they have thought about moving to Israel (the figure was 3% in a 1988 poll); at the same time 58% said that they had not thought of moving to Israel (an increase from 40% in 1988.)[27]

In France, there is broad agreement that most anti-Semitic acts have been committed by young North African Muslims. However, there is also concern that non-Muslims are increasingly engaged in anti-Semitic violence. Over the past decade, there has been a close correlation between surges in violence in the Middle East and increases in anti-Semitic acts in France. The Gulf War of 1991, the Palestinian Intifada since fall 2000, and Israeli military action on the West Bank and in Gaza since spring 2002 have all been followed by increases in anti-Semitic violence in France.[28]

The history of Jews in France is replete with important political milestones and a strong measure of controversy. In 1791, during the Revolution, France was the first European country to extend citizenship to its Jewish population. There have been three Jewish prime ministers (Léon Blum in 1936-37, Pierre Mendès-France in 1954-55, and Laurent Fabius in 1984-1986). Blum was asked by General de Gaulle to head a post-war provisional government in 1946 (he was in ill health, and declined). French Jews hold senior positions in government, business, and academics.

Some American commentators have responded to the acts of anti-Semitic violence in France by charging that the country as a whole is anti-Semitic. They see a continuity among the Dreyfus trials of the 1890s, in which a French Jewish military officer was wrongly convicted of espionage due to anti-Semitic sentiments in the government and the army, the Vichy regime of 1942-44, which collaborated with the Nazis and sent French Jews to their deaths in concentration camps, and the anti-Semitic violence that increased after 2000. They describe the strong showing of Jean-Marie Le Pen (17.85%), in the past convicted of anti-Semitic crimes by French courts, in the 2002 presidential elections as evidence that the French population retains strong anti-Semitic sentiments.[29] Israeli officials have charged that the French government's Middle East policies create an atmosphere where anti-Semitism can grow. One right-wing extremist Jewish group (*Hérout*) contends that the French government is "pro-Arab" and anti-Semitic. Some prominent French Jews intimate that the French government's criticism of Israel is a cloak for anti-Semitism.[30]

Other views contest the assertion that France is an anti-Semitic country. Charles Haddad, the president of Marseille's Jewish Council, has said, for example, that "This is not anti-Semitic violence; it's the Middle East conflict that's playing out here." Most politically moderate Jewish groups, led by the Representative Council of French Jewish Organizations (CRIF), have stated that they do not regard the general French population as anti-Semitic. They have also commended the French government for passing a strong law (the Lellouche Law) in December 2002 that cracks down on anti-Semitic violence and other racist crimes. There is no evidence that members of President Chirac's government have anti-Semitic views. President Chirac and other members of his government have vigorously condemned anti-Semitism, and held a number of public events criticizing such acts. David Harris, the executive director of the American Jewish Committee, has commended the French government for its efforts.[31]

ISSUES IN U.S.-FRENCH RELATIONS

European Security and Defense Policy (ESDP)

In the 1990s, the EU began to implement a Common Foreign and Security Policy (CFSP) to express common goals and interests on selected issues and to strengthen its influence in world affairs. Since 1999, with France playing a key role, the EU has attempted to develop a defense identity outside NATO to provide military muscle to CFSP. The European Security and Defense Policy (ESDP) is the project that gives shape to this effort. Under ESDP, the EU is creating a rapid reaction force of 60,000 troops and institutional links to NATO to prevent duplication of resources.[32] Since January 2003, the EU has launched several police and military missions under ESDP in the Balkans, and led a small international peacekeeping mission in the Congo, which France headed.

Recently, France and Germany, with some support from Britain, have sought to enhance EU decision-making bodies and a planning staff for EU military forces under ESDP. The Bush Administration opposed elements of this effort, particularly the proposal for a planning staff, as duplicative of NATO structures and a waste of resources. Some U.S. officials believe that France has actively sought to undermine NATO and to reduce U.S. influence in Europe by strengthening ESDP. French officials strongly deny such allegations. On December 12, 2003, NATO and the EU reached a compromise. There will be two planning staffs, with officers from EU states forming an EU planning cell at NATO's Supreme Headquarters Allied Command Europe (SHAPE) in Mons, Belgium, and NATO officers will be attached to a new, separate EU planning cell. U.S. officials continue to express concern that the EU planning cell, although small, will grow in time to compete with the NATO planning staff. The EU-NATO agreement reaffirms elements of an existing arrangement (called "Berlin Plus"), under which the EU will consider undertaking operations only if NATO as a whole has decided not to be engaged. If NATO is engaged, then the EU will not seek to duplicate NATO's operational planning capabilities.[33] The arrangement is intended to meet the U.S. concern that there not be two existing, and potentially competing, plans for an operation.

French officials respond to U.S. criticisms of ESDP in part by saying that the project does not compete with NATO. In the French view, there are too many crises and a shortage of capable forces in Europe and the United States to manage them. French and other European officials buttress this argument by noting the apparent shortage of forces for simultaneous stability operations in Afghanistan, the Balkans, and Iraq. U.S. officials concede that France and Britain are the only two NATO allies with flexible combat forces able to travel long distances and sustain themselves. EU defense ministers, under a plan offered by France, Britain, and Germany, agreed in April 2004 to create up to nine "battle groups" of 1,500 troops each to act as "insertion forces" in the beginning stages of a crisis. Under this plan, the forces would also be available to NATO. If brought to fruition, the battle groups would be in action within 15 days of a decision to use them, and could sustain themselves for four months before a larger force replaces them.[34]

ESDP remains a work in progress. The EU includes several self-described "neutral" governments that do not have a strong interest in European defense structures. In addition, a number of governments, including several central European governments that will join the Union in May 2004, remains close to the United States and views NATO as central to their strategic interests; for the foreseeable future, these governments are unlikely to follow any effort by an EU member to distance EU defense from NATO and Washington.[35]

NATO

France joined NATO as an original member in 1949. During the early years of the Fifth Republic, President de Gaulle had a number of disputes with the United States, in part over policies, in part over the small number of Europeans in senior allied command positions. France withdrew from NATO's integrated command structure in 1966, but has retained a seat on the North Atlantic Council (NAC), the alliance's political decision-making body. Although absent from the command structure, France participates in a range of NATO military operations. There appears to be a consensus that U.S.-French military relations are excellent, despite much publicized differences between Washington and Paris on political issues.

Several factors in the 1990s contributed to renewed French doubts about NATO. Some French officials did not want the United States exercising strong leadership in the alliance when Washington appeared to be giving Europe diminished priority after the Cold War. U.S. positions on involvement in the Balkan conflicts of the early 1990s led some French and other European officials to question the alliance's efficacy, given that Europeans saw the Balkan wars as a major threat to security.[36] The United States eventually engaged its forces in the Balkans in several NATO operations, including in the Kosovo conflict in 1999.

France has approximately 4,000 soldiers engaged in NATO stabilization operations in Bosnia (SFOR) and Kosovo (KFOR). In December 2004, an EU force succeeded the NATO stabilization force in Bosnia. France will continue to play a role in the EU mission.

French officials recognize that military self-sufficiency in an era of global threats is not possible, and that EU defense efforts may eventually have a regional but not world-wide reach. Put simply, France and the EU lack the military resources to resolve major crises on their own. For these reasons, France in the last several years has become more engaged in NATO operations. For many years, French governments had opposed proposals for NATO "out-of-area" operations, meaning military operations outside the Treaty area in Europe, as well as operations beyond Europe. The crises in the former Yugoslavia in the 1990s, requiring a large military capacity to bring stability, and the September 11 attacks, requiring a military force able to sustain combat operations in a distant theater, altered French thinking. Chirac, reflecting on these developments, has said, "You have to be realistic in a changing world. We have updated our vision, which once held that NATO had geographic limits. The idea of a regional NATO no longer exists, as the alliance's involvement in Afghanistan demonstrates."[37]

Nonetheless, occasional sharp differences in NATO between Paris and Washington continue to emerge at the political level. For example, in February 2003, France (and Germany) sought to block a U.S. effort in the NAC to discuss sending NATO forces to defend Turkey in the event that the impending conflict in Iraq might spur Baghdad to strike Turkey. Paris and Berlin contended that sending forces and equipment to Turkey would amount to tacit approval of a U.S. decision to go to war, and would be a provocative act. France, and several other allies, wished instead to continue U.N. WMD weapons inspections in Iraq (discussed more fully below).

The Bush Administration reacted angrily to France's efforts in the NAC. In April 2003, Deputy Secretary of Defense Wolfowitz told the Senate Armed Services Committee that France had "created a big problem" in NATO over aid to Turkey. He would later announce the Pentagon's decision to exclude companies from France and other countries opposing the Iraq war from contracts to rebuild Iraq. Richard Perle, part of the neo-conservative movement and an advisor to the Pentagon, said, "France is no longer the ally it once was." The following month, some Senators suggested altering the NATO decision-making process to curtail France's voice.[38]

Some French officials counter that the Administration is pursuing policies that undermine the alliance and divide the Europeans. They criticize the Administration view that "the mission drives the coalition," contending that such an attitude erodes the long-held position that all member states must believe that they have a stake in allied security operations. They describe the Administration's concept for the NATO Response Force (NRF) as initially constructive, but they call into question the Administration's leadership and good faith. French officials have contended that the Administration laid the NRF on the table, told other allies to supply the forces, then stood aside. One senior French official described the U.S. attitude as, "Europeans, improve your forces, and we'll use them" which he characterized as the "practice of the toolbox."[39] In late 2004, however, the United States began to send more of its own forces to participate in the NRF.

France and Britain are the only two European allies with flexible, mobile forces that can sustain themselves long distances from their territories. In the 1990s, France began a multi-year effort to downsize and professionalize its military forces. Smaller, more flexible units were created. U.S. military officials say that French forces have improved substantially in the past decade, and have a highly educated and motivated officer corps. NATO Supreme Allied Commander Europe (SACEUR) General James Jones has said that "France probably has the military in Europe most able to deploy to distant theaters." At the same time, U.S. military officials also say that some problems persist in an overly centralized command structure, occasional poor equipment maintenance, and minimal depth in some units.

In addition to the 4,000 French troops in NATO peace operations in the Balkans, France has 540 troops (out of a total force of 6,500) in the International Security Assistance Force in Afghanistan (ISAF). In a non-NATO operation, France also has approximately 200 special forces troops that have been fighting alongside U.S. troops in Afghanistan since fall 2001 against Taliban and Al Qaeda remnants.[40]

Terrorism

Many U.S. and French officials believe that bilateral cooperation between the United States and France in law-enforcement efforts to combat terrorism since September 11 has been strong, but at the same time a range of political factors is complicating the relationship.[41] France has long experience in combating terrorism, a tightly centralized system of law enforcement, and a far-reaching network that gathers information on extremist groups. Limits on resources and important social and political issues sometimes affect elements of France's anti-terrorism policies.

Unlike the United States, France uses its military as well as the police to ensure domestic order (however, France has no equivalent of the U.S. National Guard, which can be deployed in national crises). The French military is in the midst of an effort to modify its forces to be more effective in counter-terror efforts at home and abroad.

Terrorism has an extensive history in France. Since the 1960s, terrorists have repeatedly struck French targets. Since the late 1970s, France has captured a number of members of the Basque terrorist group, the ETA, and extradited them to Spain. In recent years, a violent Corsican separatist group has carried out assassinations and bombings in France. In the past half century, France has created a number of intelligence agencies and specialized police forces to combat such groups, usually in a successful manner. In 1994, French police thwarted a hijacking at the Marseille airport; terrorists had reportedly intended to crash the plane into the Eiffel Tower. In a notable instance, in September 1995, an Algerian terrorist organization, the Armed Islamic Group (GIA), carried out bombings in the Paris subway that killed a number of French citizens. The reaction of the French government, according to U.S. and French officials, was swift, ruthless, and effective, and the bombings ceased.

Al Qaeda has carried out at least one successful attack against France. On May 6, 2002, Al Qaeda operatives exploded a car bomb in Karachi, Pakistan, that killed 11 French naval personnel. The French navy had sent men to Karachi as part of a contract to supply submarines to the Pakistani government.[42]

France has taken several steps to increase existing efforts to combat terrorism on its own soil. On September 12, 2001, France revived an existing law enforcement measure, *Vigipirate*, that enhances the ability of the government to ensure order. The government established *Vigipirate* in 1978; without legislative action, the government may activate the system. The system provides for greater surveillance of public places, government authority to cancel holidays or public gatherings that could be the target of terrorist attacks, the activation of elements of the military to secure infrastructure, and tighter security at airports, train stations, embassies, religious institutions, nuclear sites, and other locations that may come under threat. Upon activation of *Vigipirate*, the government called 35,000 personnel from the police and military to enforce such measures, including 4,000 personnel assigned to guard the Paris subway system. *Vigipirate* is still in force, although not at the highest level of alert.

Coordination has improved between the United States and France in counter-terror policy since September 11. The two governments exchange selective intelligence information on terrorist movements and financing. In January 2002, the French and U.S. governments signed an agreement allowing the U.S. Customs Service to send inspectors to the major port of Le Havre. There, U.S. inspectors have joined their French counterparts in inspecting sea cargo containers for the possible presence of weapons of mass destruction intended for shipment to U.S. ports. There is also coordination between the two governments over air travel. With some reluctance, French officials canceled several Air France flights to the United States in December 2003-January 2004, after U.S. officials told Paris that suspected terrorists might board the flights. While Paris has stated that one individual is still being sought who was on a passenger list, the French government has also said that there was no clear evidence of a planned terrorist action. The French government places air marshals on selected flights.[43]

Middle East Peace

France's long, intertwined history with the Middle East influences its debate on terrorism and its involvement in the region. While the French government supports key U.S. objectives in dismantling Al Qaeda, there is great political sensitivity in France to any issue that involves the Muslim world. A legacy of the French colonial empire is the presence of 5 to 6 million Muslims, mostly North Africans, living in France, a population that successive French governments have found difficult to integrate into society. There is tension in the French population between those of Caucasian background and those of North African origin. In a 2002 poll, 33% of those contacted believed that North Africans "cannot be integrated" into French society; 56% said that "there are too many immigrants in France."[44] Jean-Marie Le Pen, the presidential candidate for the racist National Front in the 2002 elections, appealed to such sentiments with an anti-crime platform that described "the suburbs," where most poor North Africans live, as a breeding ground for crime and terrorism. President Chirac's Gaullist Party and the leftist opposition have strongly condemned such views.

France, along with the EU and all European countries bordering the Mediterranean, views the Middle East as a neighboring region whose political developments strongly affect European affairs. For this reason, France takes a strong interest in such issues as the Middle East peace process, terrorism, and Iraq. These issues immediately arouse a debate over sensitive social questions in France.

The Road Map

French officials, and their counterparts in many EU states, are privately extremely critical of the Bush Administration's policy that, in their view, unduly favors Israel and supports an aggressive Israeli policy towards the Palestinians. France, as an EU member, takes a strong interest in the "Road Map." The EU, the United States, the U.N., and Russia developed the Road Map as a plan to encourage negotiations between Israel and the Palestinians that would lead to the creation of a Palestinian state and an end to the Israeli-Palestinian conflict. France has urged the Palestinian Authority to prevent terrorist attacks against Israel, and Israel to withdraw from settlements from Palestinian lands occupied during the 1967 war and to release political prisoners.[45]

French officials disagree with the Administration's view that the Sharon government, in using military force against the Palestinians, is striking a blow against terrorism; in contrast, they believe that the Sharon government's policy is fueling a terrorist reaction throughout the Middle East. After a meeting with the heads of state of six other EU governments in November 2001, President Chirac said that the group was unanimous in thinking that, while the Middle East conflict was not causing terrorism, "it is true that it makes it easier and creates a climate that... is favorable to Muslim extremists and fundamentalists, notably bin Laden."[46]

France joined with other EU governments in criticizing the Bush Administration's April 2004 decision to back elements of Sharon's plan to withdraw from Gaza and at the same time claim settlements for Israel on the West Bank and renounce the Palestinians' right of return to Israel. President Chirac has said that while unilateral Israeli withdrawal from Gaza was a positive step, it should be done within the process of negotiations that should lead to the creation of a Palestinian state. He has also criticized the Israeli "security fence" because it dispossesses Palestinian families of their property.[47]

France and most other EU governments believe that the Bush Administration has not worked with sufficient energy to persuade the Sharon government to negotiate peace with the Palestinians, and that the Sharon government has worked assiduously to undermine the Palestinian Authority. French officials assert that failure to negotiate with the Palestinian Authority deprives it of influence with Palestinians and encourages the ascendancy of extremist groups, such as Hamas.[48]

France has also been critical of elements of the Bush Administration's desire to promote democracy in the Middle East. In January 2005, Foreign Minister Michel Barnier criticized those who insist that there must be democracy in the region before there can be peace in the Middle East. He said that peace must come first as "an objective precondition" for democracy and reform to take hold in the region. In this view, the effort by the Bush Administration to bring democracy to Iraq in order to inspire democratic development in the rest of the Middle East is the reverse of the process that can bring reform. In Barnier's view, an Arab-Israeli peace settlement is necessary to lay the groundwork for democratic institutions.[49]

Some French observers believe that France, to protect its own interests in the Middle East, must not become too closely associated with U.S. policies there, which many Europeans see as having failed. Such a view may explain in part French opposition, and that of several other European governments, to Bush Administration efforts to develop NATO operations in Iraq.[50]

Iraq

France participated in the U.S. led Gulf War of 1991, and for several years supported the U.N. weapons inspections in Iraq. France also supported a U.N. resolution at the end of the Gulf War to prohibit the export of Iraqi oil until the Hussein regime complied with an agreement to end its WMD program.

Controversy over the Oil-for-Food Program

Over time, the United States, France, and other countries became concerned that the oil embargo was adversely affecting the conditions of the Iraqi people. In 1996, to improve humanitarian conditions in Iraq, the U.N. designed an "Oil-for-Food" program under which Iraq might export sufficient oil to feed and provide general care for its people. Almost from the beginning, there were allegations of corruption in the program. There were charges, for example, that Saddam Hussein's regime was demanding kickbacks from countries obtaining contracts to sell food and equipment under the program, and that the money was used to bribe public officials in other countries to support Iraq's cause, or to purchase illegal military equipment. U.S. representatives on the U.N. Sanctions Committee, which held oversight authority for granting contracts, were able to block any contract.[51]

Under the Oil-for-Food program, Iraqi oil exports resumed, legally, on a scale sufficient to provide humanitarian relief for the Iraqi people. France imported oil from Iraq under this program, with its highest level of imports reaching 171,000 barrels a day in 1998. However, the United States was by a wide margin the largest importer of Iraqi oil in the 1996-2001 period, purchasing approximately 60% of Iraqi exports. France was the fourth largest buyer of Iraqi oil, purchasing 8% of the crude exported by Baghdad.[52] In both the U.S. and French cases, the transactions were legal.

Some Members of Congress have questioned whether some governments, including the French government, opposed the U.S. use of force against Iraq in the winter and spring of 2002-2003 out of concern that the overthrow of Hussein would expose corrupt practices under the Oil-for-Food program. In this view, "corruption on this scale carries with it the potential to skew international decision-making." On April 7, 2004, then U.S. ambassador to the U.N. John Negroponte testified before the Senate Foreign Relations Committee that France, China, and Russia may have been unwilling to impose stricter sanctions guidelines under the Oil-for-Food program out of concern that such corruption might have been uncovered.

Conversely, a Department of Defense audit did not support the allegation that the French government or French companies may have benefitted from the Oil-for-Food program in any substantial way. It found that 70% of the kickbacks and overpricing involved companies from eight countries. France was not named as one of those countries, according to the audit. The Duelfer report on WMD in Iraq touched upon corruption in the Oil-for-Food program. It did mention that "entities" from Russia, China, and France may have received kickbacks from Iraq under the program. It listed French companies and individuals that may have received such kickbacks. The report acknowledged that several U.S. companies may also have received kickbacks, but the report did not name them out of concern for "privacy." This statement led the French government to cry foul. Why, it asked, did the report name French entities, but apply a different standard to U.S. companies?[53]

France has opened a judicial investigation of possible kickbacks to the oil company Total. Paris contends that there is no evidence that possible corruption influences French policy.[54]

There is an investigation underway at the United Nations on corruption in the Oil-for-Food program, to which France has reportedly supplied requested documents. The Bush Administration acknowledges that the French government fully supports the investigation. French officials have strongly denied any wrongdoing on the part of their government, and say that the investigation should uncover whether any French companies acted illegally. The French ambassador to the United States has noted that the U.S. government, having a seat on the U.N. Sanctions Committee, reviewed all applications by French companies for contracts and had the authority to veto any of them. Some were in fact vetoed, on the basis that the contracts were for dual-use items prohibited for import by Iraq. According to one source, 93 of 184 contracts for sale of dual-use items to Iraq by French companies were vetoed.[55] It is unclear whether any contracts might have been vetoed out of concern over kickbacks, an issue that may be resolved by the U.N. investigation.

The Iraq War of 2003

During the late 1990s, the French government began to distance itself from elements of U.S. policy in Iraq when the United States and Britain resorted to occasional military force to persuade the Hussein regime to comply with elements of the settlement that concluded the 1991 Gulf War. U.N. weapons inspectors left Iraq in 1998, when international will to enforce the inspection regime weakened. France, along with other governments, expressed concern that living conditions in Iraq were deteriorating, and sought to lift international sanctions against the Hussein regime. Both the Clinton Administration and the Bush Administration strongly opposed such a move.

When the Bush Administration took office, it quickly raised the level of U.S. criticism over Iraq's opposition to U.N. inspections for weapons of mass destruction. In fall 2002, after some hesitation, France backed the U.S. effort to reinstate U.N. weapons inspections. U.N. Resolution 1441 required Iraq to comply with the inspections. In late 2002 and early 2003, the Bush Administration stated that Iraq was impeding the inspections and concealing WMD, and was thereby in "material breach" of Resolution 1441. In the Administration's view, breach of the Resolution's requirements justified further action, including the possible use of military force, to ensure compliance. The French government, backed by Germany, which had joined the U.N. Security Council in January 2003 as a rotating member, contended that while Iraq was not in full compliance with Res. 1441, it was not yet in "material breach" of the Resolution's strictures. The French government wished for the inspections to continue, asserting that there was as yet no clear evidence that WMD was being concealed. Privately, some French officials were saying that Iraq likely had concealed WMD, but that the inspections regime was sufficient to constrain Saddam's regime.[56]

A crucial period in the U.S.-French dispute over Iraq came in February and March 2003. In February 2003 the Administration circulated drafts of a resolution at the U.N. that would have permitted military action against Iraq. While the U.N. Security Council had agreed to inspections for WMD, the

Administration began to add additional ideas. Administration officials called for "regime change" in Iraq, and the establishment of a democracy that would serve as a model and a spur for new representative governments throughout the Middle East. France and other governments balked at these added objectives, asserting that sustainable reforms in Iraq and elsewhere could not be imposed by others.

The Administration also asked that NATO begin planning to provide Turkey with defensive systems in the event of an attack by Iraq in an impending conflict. In addition, the request asked that NATO members backfill for some U.S. forces in the Balkans, that might be needed in the event of conflict with Iraq. France, Germany, and Belgium, objected in the North Atlantic Council (NAC), NATO's supreme political body. They contended that granting the request would be the equivalent of acknowledging that Iraq had impeded U.N. weapons inspections, as yet unproven in the view of the three governments, and be a pretext for war. Ultimately, the German and Belgian governments relented, and France agreed that the decision to aid Turkey could be taken in another NATO body where Paris is not a member. The result in late February 2003 was a decision to provide defensive assistance to Turkey. This dispute generated calls in Congress that NATO decision-making be altered to exclude France, and fueled a popular barrage of U.S. criticism against France and several other allies. Secretary of Defense Rumsfeld began to refer to a "new" Europe of countries that supported the U.S. position on Iraq, and an "old" Europe of countries such as France and Germany that opposed U.S. policy.[57]

However, France and Germany would not relent in their opposition to the Administration's draft U.N. resolution authorizing the possible use of force against Iraq. France and Russia, each holding a veto, threatened to use it if the resolution were submitted to a vote. Then foreign minister de Villepin said, "We think that a military intervention would be the worst solution and that a recourse to force should be the last path...." He added that only the U.N. could authorize an invasion.[58]

In March 2003, the Bush Administration decided to go to war in Iraq without a new U.N. resolution. Several key allies, led by France and Germany, with indirect support from Turkey, opposed the decision. Other allies, led by Britain, Italy, Poland, and Spain, backed the Administration.

U.S. forces overthrew Saddam Hussein's regime in April 2003. The Administration has sought to gather an international coalition to stabilize Iraq. France put forward requirements to be fulfilled before Paris would provide military forces or other forms of assistance in Iraq. The French government criticized the U.S. description of the coalition's presence in Iraq as an "occupation," without a detailed plan and timetable for ending the occupation and turning sovereignty over to the Iraqi people. In September 2003, Chirac said, "It is very difficult for the Iraqis to accept a situation which, in one way or another, is one of occupation. The situation can only deteriorate."[59] De Villepin called for "a rapid transfer of sovereignty...." The answer to the problems in Iraq is not more troops, he continued, but a "true provisional government whose legitimacy will be underpinned by the U.N. and will benefit from the support of the countries of the region." There must be, in the French view, he continued, a U.N. resolution that would endorse such an arrangement.[60]

In fall 2003, the situation in Iraq began to deteriorate, under the impetus of a gathering insurgency. Diplomatic efforts at the U.N. and in the alliance to develop more support for U.S. policy in Iraq continued. In December 2003, Deputy Defense Secretary Wolfowitz issued an order that stated that governments not involved in the coalition in Iraq would see their companies excluded from competition for contracts to rebuild the country, a step that he described as being "necessary for the protection of the essential security interests of the United States...."[61]

Simultaneously, the Administration asked France and Germany, two governments excluded from such competition, to agree to restructure their debt with Iraq. France accepted a U.S.-German compromise plan negotiated in the context of the Paris Club to write off 80% of Iraq's foreign debt; this percentage is higher than the 50% of debt forgiveness that Paris had advocated, although it falls short of original U.S. requests for nearly complete debt forgiveness for Iraq. In France's view, Iraq retains the potential for great wealth from its petroleum resources, and other, poorer countries would more clearly benefit from debt forgiveness. Iraq owes France $3 billion, Germany $2.4 billion, and the United States $2 billion.[62]

The French government has refused to send forces to be part of the U.S.-led multinational force in Iraq. French officials say that Paris did not approve the conditions under which the United States launched the war and does not wish to be associated with the occupation of Iraq. At the NATO summit in June 2004, France and several other allies initially opposed sending a NATO force to Iraq. Chirac said that "any involvement of NATO in [the Middle East] seems to us to carry great risks, including the risk of confrontation of the Christian West against the Muslim East."

Ultimately, all allies agreed upon a training mission, but some countries do not wish to send their forces to Iraq to train Iraqi security forces. France was one of these countries, but has offered to train Iraqi police in metropolitan France.[63]

Trade[64]

U.S. commercial ties with France are extensive, mutually profitable, and growing. With approximately $1 billion in commercial transactions taking place between the two countries *every business day* of the year, each country has an increasingly large stake in the health and openness of the other's economy.

France is the 9th largest merchandise trading partner for the United States and the United States is France's largest trading partner outside the European Union. In 2003, 64% or $29.7 billion of bilateral trade occurred in major industries such as aerospace, pharmaceuticals, medical and scientific equipment, electrical machinery, and plastics where both countries export and import similar products. Many of these products are components or capital goods used in the production of finished products in both the United States and France.

The United States and France also have a large and growing trade in services such as tourism, education, finance, insurance and other professional services. In 2002, France was the sixth largest market for U.S. exports of services and the seventh largest provider of services to the United States.

While trade in goods and services receives most of the attention in terms of the commercial relationship, foreign direct investment and the activities of foreign affiliates can be viewed as the backbone of the commercial relationship. The scale of sales of U.S.-owned companies operating in France and French-owned companies operating in the United States outweighs trade transactions by a factor of *six* to *five*.

In 2002 France was the sixth largest host country for U.S. foreign direct investment abroad and the United States with investments valued at $43.9 billion (historical cost basis) was the number one foreign investor in France. During that same year, French companies had direct investments in the United States totaling $171 billion (historical cost basis), making France the second largest investor in the United States. French-owned companies employed some 578,600 workers in the United States in 2001 compared to 540,000 employees of U.S. companies invested in France.

Most U.S. trade and investment transactions with France, dominated by multinational companies, are non-controversial. Nevertheless, three prominent issues — agriculture, government intervention in corporate activity, and the war in Iraq —have contributed to increased bilateral tensions in recent years.

Agriculture

Agricultural trade disputes historically have been the major sticking point in U.S.-France commercial relations. Although the agricultural sector accounts for a declining percentage of output and employment in both countries, it has produced a disproportionate amount of trade tensions between the two sides.

From the U.S. perspective, the restrictive trade regime set up by the Common Agricultural Policy (CAP) has been the real villain. It has been a longstanding U.S. contention that the CAP is the largest single distortion of global agricultural trade. American farmers and policymakers have complained over the years that U.S. sales and profits are adversely affected by (1) EU restrictions on market access that have protected the European market for European farmers; by (2) EU export subsidies that have deflated U.S. sales to third markets; and by (3) EU domestic income support programs that have kept non-competitive European farmers in business.

France's agricultural sector, which in terms of output and land is the largest in Europe, has long been the biggest beneficiary of the CAP. In 2002, French farmers received 9.8 billion euros in CAP subsidies out of a total EU outlay of 43.2 billion euros.[65] Acting to continue benefits and subsidies for its farmers, the French position can determine the limits and parameters of the European Commission's negotiating flexibility on a range of agricultural issues that are of keen interest to the United States. The most prominent and perhaps important example relates to current efforts to get the WTO Doha round of multilateral trade negotiations back on track by reducing agricultural subsidies. While the European Commission on May 10, 2004 offered to eliminate $3.3 billion in export subsidies, François Loos, the French trade minister, balked on the grounds that the commission exceeded its mandate.[66] Other examples where the French position arguably has made settlement of disputes more difficult include expanded trademark protection for wines, cheeses, and other food products linked to specific regions, limits on research and use of genetically-modified (GM) crops, and a ban on the importation of beef treated with hormones.[67]

Government Intervention in Corporate Activity

Despite significant reform and privatization over the past 15 years, the center-right French government continues to play a larger role in influencing corporate activity than does the U.S. government. This difference is manifested not only in the French government's continuing direct control of key companies, but also in its continuing proclivity to influence mergers involving French firms. The French government's close corporate ties have also embroiled it in embarrassing disclosures related to an on-going investigation of Credit Lyonnais's 12-year old acquisition of a California insurance company. Nevertheless, although bilateral disputes may be more prone to occur because of the French government's interventionist tendencies, the dictates of EU laws as well as the urgent need to raise the revenues that accompany privatization efforts, are weakening the French *dirigiste* tradition.

The most recent example of French government intervention in the marketplace centered on the creation of a national pharmaceuticals champion. It did this in April 2004 by publicly backing the merger of Sanofi-Synthelabo, a Paris-based pharmaceuticals company, with Aventis, a French-German competitor. The merger will make Sanofi-Aventis the world's third largest drug company, behind a U.S. company, Pfizer, and a U.K. company, GlaxoSmithKline. By opposing a rival bid and approach by the Swiss-based Novartis Group, the French government, according to critics, reinforced the belief that it plays a big role in all economic decisions in the French market. Prime Minister Jean-Pierre Raffarin countered that "this does not mean France will be nationalistic, individualistic and egotistical, but will be open to projects with our European and other partners."[68] Nevertheless, the message that the current government, like many of its predecessors, intends to play an active role in the economy that on occasion may favor national control of business may not be lost on foreign investors.[69]

The French government's longstanding propensity to intervene in the marketplace also is related, in part, to the on-going scandal and litigation involving the French bank Credit Lyonnais. In the early 1990s, Credit Lyonnais, then a huge state-owned bank, violated certain U.S. laws in an effort to purchase Executive Life, a failed California-based insurance company. In January of 2004, the French government was forced to plead guilty in U.S. District Court in California to fraud and French taxpayers had to pay $375 million of the $770 million criminal case fines. In a larger civil lawsuit that is scheduled for trial in February 2005, California's insurance regulator is seeking up to $5 billion in damages.[70]

Foreign Policy Discord

In the era of the Cold War, there was considerable concern that trade disputes between allies could undermine political and security ties. Deep differences over the Iraq war between the United States and many of its allies, particularly France and Germany, reversed this Cold War concern into whether foreign policy disputes can weaken or undermine strong commercial ties.

Specific concerns that divisions over Iraq could spill over into the trade arena arose in early 2003 with reports of U.S. consumer boycotts of French goods and calls from some U.S. lawmakers for trade retaliation against France (and Germany). The spike in bilateral tensions and hard feelings, however, appears *not* to have had much impact on sales of the products — such as wines, perfumes, handbags, and cheeses — most prone to being boycotted.[71] While total U.S. imports from France increased by 3.5% in 2002/2003, U.S. imports of wine increased by 21.5%, imports of perfumes and toiletries by 17.8%, imports of travel goods and handbags by 31.3%, and imports of cheese and curd by 20.0%. All four categories also increased their share of total imports.[72]

While there are few signs that goods and services clearly identified with France or the United States are being boycotted, some polls have found evidence of public support among some segments of the U.S. population for expressing opposition to foreign policy disagreements in the shopping malls. Nevertheless, a substantial economic backlash appears unlikely due to the high degree of economic integration. Effective boycotts would jeopardize thousands of jobs on both sides of the Atlantic.

ASSESSMENT

The United States and France retain a strong measure of economic and political interdependence. In economic terms, some $360 billion in annual commercial transactions, the vast majority due to sales by U.S. companies producing and selling in France and French companies producing and selling in the United States, serves as a strong form of economic glue that binds the two countries together. This deep and growing level of economic integration increases the stakes each country has in the vitality and openness of each other's economy, as well as works as a counterweight to the adoption of restrictive policies which could jeopardize hundreds of thousands of jobs in both countries. In political terms, France acknowledges the security that only U.S. forces can provide on a global scale, evident in the conflict against terrorism and the post-September 11 campaign to overthrow the Taliban and weaken Al Qaeda. The United States also plays a key institutional role in stabilizing Europe, a measure of which is Washington's leadership in enlarging NATO.

Additionally, France does act to buttress U.S. international efforts and to lend legitimacy to Washington's foreign policy initiatives, measures that demonstrate a complementarity of interests and action that is still the norm, even if at times that norm appears to be diminishing. French forces fought in the Gulf War of 1991, and, with much greater ability, in the Kosovo conflict of 1999. France has followed important U.S. initiatives that seek to enhance global stability, as in NATO's eventual acceptance of the once controversial idea that NATO go "out of area," and act on a global scale. In the conflict against terrorism, France has supplied the Bush Administration with political contacts in countries, such as Algeria and Tunisia, that have proven valuable.[73] With other EU countries, France has worked closely with the United States in law enforcement efforts to combat terrorism.

Important divergences have emerged over the past decade. The belief in France that the United States at times acts "unilaterally" was already evident in the 1990s when the French government criticized Congress and the Clinton Administration for defeat of the Comprehensive Test Ban Treaty, sanctions against Cuba, and a program of national missile defense.[74] This belief has sharpened during the current Bush Administration, due to its rejection of the Kyoto Treaty, its criticism of the International Criminal Court, and its Iraq policy. French public opinion has grown increasingly critical of the United States since late 2002. In October 2001, shortly after the terrorist attacks on the United States, 67% of those polled had a favorable opinion of the United States; in May 2004, that figure had slipped to 34%. In October 2001, 53% of those polled had "confidence in the United States to deal responsibly with world affairs;" by May 2004, that figure had fallen to 13%.[75]

France's belief in the importance of international institutions is deeply ingrained, a sentiment shared not only by such traditional U.S. allies as Germany and Britain, but learned and accepted as well by the democracies that have emerged from the Warsaw Pact. The United States is in part responsible for this belief. After the Second World War, Washington strongly urged acceptance of international institutions to resolve disputes and manage global financial and economic systems. Since the end of the Cold War, a centerpiece of the policy of three U.S. Administrations has been that central European governments should join NATO, the European Union, and other institutions as a means to ensure stability through closer consultation, joint decision-making, and development of interdependence. Many European governments have embraced these institutions as an antidote to the conflicts of the 20th century.

The continuing controversy over Iraq illustrates the divergence between the United States and France over the use of international institutions and military force. Regarding the former, President Bush challenged the U.N. in fall 2002 to meet its responsibilities and enforce the U.N. prohibition on weapons of mass destruction in Iraq. He noted that the difficult tasks undertaken by the U.N., such as those involving the threat or use of military force and the consequent expending of resources, often fell to major governments, such as the United States. The French government, and other allies, were ultimately sympathetic to this argument, and backed a new effort to enforce inspections. When the Bush Administration began to criticize the inspections regime as insufficient several weeks after its inception, France, joined by Germany and several other allies, asked for time, and noted privately that it was Washington, after all, that was supplying much of the information to the U.N. for site inspections. They wished to allow the inspections to run their course. French officials also feared that war in Iraq could trigger unintended consequences, such as prolonged conflict or destabilization of neighboring regions, and an expansion of global terrorism.[76]

Differences over Iraq also threatened in early 2003 to disrupt commercial ties with reports of U.S. consumer boycotts of French goods. U.S. companies too worried that French and other European consumers might not buy their products as a way of expressing opposition to U.S. policy. Despite public opinion surveys indicating some support for using the marketplace to demonstrate political dissatisfaction, there is little evidence that sales so far have been adversely affected due to the foreign policy discord on either side of the Atlantic.

A complementarity of interests and action in many spheres is likely to continue. For those in Congress and in the executive branch who desire greater European burdensharing in the alliance, ESDP holds at least the possibility of greater military capability among continental allies, a capability that could be used by NATO for conflicts in the region, or in more distant theaters. For those who desire greater contributions by other countries in peacekeeping, or in international financial institutions, French influence and policy often buttress U.S. interests and diminish the need for greater expenditure of U.S. resources. And for those who desire to maintain an open world trading system, the French support in the councils of the European Union and World Trade Organization is sometimes critical.

Finally, France and the United States, while sharing values inherent in most democratic societies, will likely continue to have different political perspectives, particularly over the role of international institutions and the use of force. French efforts to build a politically strengthened EU and an effective ESDP could reduce the U.S. role and influence on the continent. Some critics of France have interpreted instances of disagreement as a desire on the part of France to see the United States fail. However, failure of the United States in areas of foreign affairs would have direct implications for France and other European countries. In Iraq, failure of the U.S. effort to bring stability, for example, has potentially great negative consequences for all Europeans: further disaffection with U.S. leadership of NATO; a renewal of radical Islam in the Middle East, with regimes hostile to western governments; and further exacerbation of tensions in the Middle East, with unwanted consequences on the European continent.

REFERENCES

[1]   Anand Menon, France, *NATO and the Limits of Independence, 1981-1997: The Politics of Ambivalence* (New York, St. Martin's Press, 2000), p. 69-71.

[2]   "U.N. is wary of dangers in taking lead role in Iraq," *New York Times* (NYT), April 18, 2004, p. 8.

[3]   "U.S. French 'marriage' edgy but still there...," *Rocky Mountain News*, (interview with Ambassador Jean-David Levitte), April 15, 2004, p. 41A.

[4]   French-owned companies operating in the United States and U.S.-owned companies operating in France directly employ over 1.2 million persons and bilateral merchandise trade flows create an estimated 500,000 jobs (based on the Department of Commerce estimate that every $1 billion in exports creates 10,000 jobs). This CRS estimate of 1.7 million jobs does not include jobs associated with the $20 billion in trade in services between the two countries.

[5]   In a vast literature, see John Weightman, "Fatal Attraction," *New York Review of Books* (NYR). Feb. 11, 1993, p. 10; and François Furet, *La Révolution de Turgot à Jules Ferry, 1770-1880* (Paris, 1988), p. 511-512, 516-517.

[6]   The term "Gaullist" originated during Charles de Gaulle's presidency (1958-1969). President Chirac was a founder of the Gaullist Party, once known as the Rally for the Republic. Gaullists have traditionally

believed in a strong national voice and an independent foreign policy for France, and that France must play a central role in shaping Europe and in influencing world affairs. Gaullists are also normally fiscal conservatives who have supported a statist position in the economy; some current Gaullists support elements of privatization in the French economy.

[7]   EU: Report examines countries' views on IGC issues. FBIS-WEU-96-052. March 15, 1996, p. 11; and "Débat au Sénat sur la CIG: Intervention du Ministre des Affaires Etrangères M. de Charette." March 14, 1996, unpaginated text.

[8]   De Villepin cited by Daniel Vernet, "Dominique de Villepin ou le gaullisme ressucité," *Le Monde* (LM), Dec. 11, 2003. De Villepin is now the Interior Minister. Thierry Tardy, "France and the United States: the inevitable clash?," *International Journal,* vol. LIX, no. 1, winter 2003-2004.

[9]   Christoph Bertram, in "La diplomatie Villepin jugée par les intellectuels," *LM*, Dec. 4, 2003, p. 16; interviews.

[10] "Le Premier choix de Paris reste la relation avec Berlin," LM, Feb. 18, 2004, p. 2; "Après le fiasco de Bruxelles, Paris relance l'idée d'une Europe à la carte," *LM*, Dec. 16, 2003, p. 10.

[11] Discussions with French officials, 2003-2005; "Après le fiasco de Bruxelles...," *op. cit.*

[12] "En 2003, les six instants qui ont mis la France en délicatesse avec l'Europe," *LM*, Jan. 1, 2004, p. 6; interviews, 2003-March 2004. Romania and Bulgaria hope to join the EU in 2007.

[13] Interviews; "EU scolds France on budget discipline," *International Herald Tribune (IHT)*, Jan. 29, 2004, p. 11.

[14] *Interviews with Polish, Romanian, Hungarian, and Czech officials*, Feb. 2003-April 2004.

[15] De Villepin, "Discours d'ouverture," Meeting of French ambassadors, Ministry of Foreign Affairs, Paris, Aug. 28, 2003; and Jacques Chirac, Speech before the U.N. General Assembly, excerpted in *LM*, Sept. 24, 2003, p. 2.

[16] *Interviews and discussions with U.S. and French officials*, February-March 1999.

[17] Cited in "New year, old theme: Chirac elbows Bush," NYT, Jan. 10-11, 2004; and "L'Amérique ne comprend pas qu'elle ait été jugée 'plus dangereuse que Saddam Hussein,'" *LM*, June 1-2, 2003, p. 3 (interview with Rice).

[18] See Charles Krauthammer, "The Unipolar Moment Revisited," National Interest, winter 2002/2003; "France may pose long-term challenge to U.S. defense policy, Perle says," *Aerospace Daily*, Feb. 13, 2003, p. 4-5.

[19] Menon, *op. cit.*, p. 69-70.

[20] "New Year...," *op. cit.*; De Villepin, "Discours...," *op. cit.*

[21] For a discussion, see Justin Vaïsse, "*Veiled meaning: the French law banning religious symbols in public schools*," Brookings Institution, March 2004. For the French government's view, see "*Laïcité in France: Promoting Religious Freedom and Tolerance*," supplied by the French embassy, March 2004.

[22] Vaïsse, *op. cit.*, p. 3.

[23] Cited in "French premier urges approval of scarf ban," *IHT*, Feb. 4, 2004, p. 3.

[24] Vaïsse, *op. cit.*, p. 5.

[25] Jean Baubérot, "Laïcité, le grand écart," (editorial), *LM*, Jan. 4-5, 2004, p. 1.

[26] "Jacques Chirac remobilise le gouvernement contre l'antisémitisme," *LM*, Nov. 18, 2003.

[27] "Qui sont les juifs de France?", *Le Figaro*, Nov. 18, 2002.

[28] "Les Juifs et les Arabes en France," Le Nouvel Observateur, Jan. 24-30, 2002, p. 5; "Wave of anti-Semitism called threat to France," *IHT*, Oct. 20, 2004, p. 3.

[29] See, for example, Charles Krauthammer, "Europe and 'those people': anti-Semitism rises again," *Washington Post* (WP), April 26, 2002, p. A29. Most analysts believe that Le Pen's strong showing was due to his attacks on immigrants and crime, and not to his anti-Semitic views.

[30] "Les Juifs et les Arabes...," op. cit.; "Les Juifs de France et la France, une confiance à rétablir," editorial by several members of French Jewish community, *LM*, Dec. 30, 2003, p. 1.

[31] For Haddad, see "Attacks on Jews leave Marseille wondering about a rupture," *NYT*, April 8, 2002, p. 2; "Les clés d'une débâcle," Libération, April 24, 2002, p. 1; "Chirac remobilise...," op. cit.; and [letter from David Harris], "Anti-Semitism in France," *IHT*, Jan 7, 2003, p. 7.

[32] For a more detailed analysis, see CRS Report RL32342, *NATO and the European Union*, by Kristin Archick and Paul Gallis.

[33] *Interviews*, Nov. 2003-Jan; 2005; Statement of (then) NATO Secretary General Robertson, cited in *Atlantic News*, Dec. 17, 2003.

[34] Interviews, Dec. 2003-Jan. 2005; "Battle Group plan advances," *IHT*, April 6, 2004, p. 3.

[35] *Interviews*, 2003-2005.

[36] For a thought-provoking discussion, see Menon, *op. cit.*

[37] Jim Hoagland, "Chirac's multipolar world," *WP*, Feb. 4, 2004, p.A22 (editorial based on an interview with Chirac).

[38] Hearing. Senate Armed Services Committee, 108th Congress, 1st sess., April 10, 2003; Perle cited in Stacy Schiff (ed.), "Vive l'Histoire," *NYT*, Feb. 6, 2003, p. A35; *Congressional Record*, May 7, 2003, p. S5818-5824.

[39] *Interviews*, Nov. 2003-Jan. 2005; "*The Military role in Countering Terrorism at Home and Abroad: U.S. and French Approaches*," conference of U.S. and French officials, Nov. 20-22, 2003. At one point, France had the largest contingent — 2,000 troops in a total NRF of 6,000. The Administration counters that the NRF was designated as a force to be initially filled out by Europeans so that the allies could demonstrate a commitment to building more flexible, mobile forces.

[40] *Interviews with U.S. officials 2003-2005*; "A l'OTAN, des responsables américains louent le savoir-faire de l'armée française," *LM*, Oct. 9, 2003, p. 5; "*Fact sheet on French armed forces*," July 2004, provided by the Embassy of France, Washington.

[41] This section is an abbreviated, updated version of the section on France in CRS Report RL31612, *European Counterterrorist Efforts since September 11: Political Will and Diverse Responses*, coordinated by Paul Gallis. The study was originally prepared as a memorandum for Representative Doug Bereuter and the House Select Committee on Intelligence, and became a CRS report with Mr. Bereuter's permission.

[42] "Face au terrorisme, M. Chirac prend seul la tête de l'executif," *LM*, May 10, 2002, p. 2.

[43] "Terrorisme: Français et Américains se félicitent de leur coopération en matière de renseignement," *LM*, Dec. 31, 2003, p. 5; "France has no evidence of bomb plot," *IHT*, Jan. 9, 2004, p. 3; interviews.

[44] Ariane Chebel D'Appollonia, "*The National Front and anti-Semitism in France*, " Center on the United States and France, Brookings Institution, July 2002.

[45] De Villepin, "Discours d'ouverture," *op. cit.*

[46] "Les dirigeants européens soulignent les limites de l'action militaire," *LM*, Nov. 6, 2001, p. 4.

[47] "Point de presse conjoint de M. Jacques Chirac...et de M. Hosni Mubarak...," French Ministry of Foreign Affairs, April 19, 2004; "Jacques Chirac: 'pas conforme au droit international,'" *LM*, Feb. 14, 2004, p. 2.

[48] "Gaza pullout is endorsed, with proviso, by envoys," *NYT*, May 5, 2004, p. A8.

[49] "A French call for a new day with U.S.," *IHT*, Jan. 10, 2005, p. 1.

[50] François Heisbourg, "Accablant 6 juin 2004," *LM*, June 5, 2004, p. 1.

[51] For an analysis of the overall program, see CRS Report RL30472, *Iraq: Oil-for-Food Program, International Sanctions, and Illicit Trade*, by Kenneth Katzman.

[52] Energy Information Administration, U.S. Dept. of Energy, January 2003; "Les échanges franco-irakiens ont triplé depuis 1997," *LM*, Jan. 4, 2003, p. 2; "Un changement de régime en Irak coûtera cher à la France," *La Tribune*, Feb. 5, 2003, p. 1.

[53] "Hussein used oil to dilute sanctions," *WP*, Oct. 7, 2004, p. A1; "*Statement by the Ambassador of France to the United States on the Oil for Food program*," Embassy of France, Washington, Oct. 7, 2004.

[54] "U.N. Oil-for-Food Program," Senate Foreign Relations Committee, hearing, 108th Congress, 2nd session, April 7, 2004; "L'enquête sur Total conduit à des soupçons de caisse noire et de corruption," *LM*, Oct. 16, 2004, p. 10.

[55] "U.S.-French 'marriage' edgy but still there," *Rocky Mountain News*, (interview with Ambassador Jean-David Levitte), April 15, 2004, p. 41A; "Eurobiz is caught arming Saddam," *Insight on the News*, Feb. 18-March 3, 2003.

[56] Tardy, *op. cit.*, p. 6-7; *interviews*, Nov. 2002-Feb. 2003.

[57] CRS Report RS21510, *NATO's Decision-Making Procedure*, by Paul Gallis.

[58] "Le 'non' de Paris, au prix d'une grave crise," *LM*, Dec. 28-29, 2003, p. III; Tardy, op. cit., p. 7.

[59] "Paris-Washington, deux diagnostics opposés sur la situation en Irak," *LM*, Sept. 25, 2003, p. 2.

[60] De Villepin, "Discours d'ouverture," (*conference of ambassadors at the Ministry of Foreign Affairs*, Paris), Aug. 28, 2003.

[61] Deputy Secretary of Defense Wolfowitz, "*Determinations and Findings,*" Dept. of Defense, Dec. 5, 2003.

[62]   "Give me liberty or give me debt," (ed.) *Financial Times* (FT), June
       10, 2004, p. 14; and "French president spells out limits on Iraq
       support," *FT*, June 11, 2004, p. 6.

[63]   Interviews of U.S. officials, July 2004; "Allies to support Iraq with
       troop training," NATO, Brussels, June 29, 2004; "Paris et Washington
       s'affrontent sur le rôle de l'OTAN en Irak," *LM*, June 26, 2004, p. 2.

[64]   This section is drawn from CRS Report RL32459, *U.S.-French
       Commercial Ties,* by Raymond J. Ahearn.

[65]   European Commission, Directorate for Agriculture, Financial Report
       2002. Found at [*http://europa.eu.int/comm/agriculture/agrista/2003/
       table_en/342.pdf*].

[66]   Meller, Paul. "France Splits With Europe Over Farm Subsidy Plan,"
       NYT, May 11, 2004, p. W1. Some observers argue that French
       opposition to reform is often tactical and that it has not prevented
       substantial reform of the CAP.

[67]   Trademark protection for geographic indications is also an issue of
       great importance for Italy (parma ham and parmesan cheese), Greece
       (feta cheese), Hungary (tokay wine), and Portugal (porto wine).
       Denmark, Italy, and Germany are other EU countries taking the lead
       on limits on research and use of GM crops and most all EU members
       strongly support the ban on the importation of beef treated with
       hormones. For further discussion of these disputes, see CRS Report
       RS21569, *Geographical Indications and WTO Negotiations*, by
       Charles Hanrahan, CRS ebtra53, *Biotechnology and Agricultural
       Trade*, by Geoffrey Becker and Charles Hanrahan, and CRS Report
       RL31841, *Agricultural Trade Issues in the 108th Congress*, by
       Geoffrey Becker and Charles Hanrahan.

[68]   Johnson, Jo, "Deal is a setback to investment," *FT*, April 27, 2004, p.
       18.

[69]   France's newly appointed Finance Minister, Nicolas Sarkozy, in his
       first news conference, called for relaxation of EU state-aid rules to
       allow national governments to expend public funds on enhancing the
       competitiveness of key companies. See Bennhold, Katrin, " Sarkozy
       Urges Europe to Forge Industrial Hubs," *IHT*, May 5, 2004, p.1.

[70]   Carreyrou, John and Glenn R. Simpson, "Foreign Policy: How
       Insurance Spat Further Frayed U.S.-French Ties — Paris Forks Over
       $375 Million in Executive Life Dispute; Gucci Owner Pinned Down
       — California's Civil Suit Looms," *The Wall Street Journal*, April 16,
       2004.

[71] This is an illustrative, not exhaustive, list of products that are likely to be targets of boycotts because they have a strong element of brand identification with France, and tend to be luxury items.

[72] In January-February 2004, total U.S. imports from France were down 1.76% over January-February 2003, but three of the four categories experienced healthy growth with perfumes up 13.1%, travel goods up 5.5%, and cheese and curd up 25.5%. Wine imports, however, were down 4.7% over the January/February 2003 level.

[73] "Hubert Védrine effectue une tournée éclair au Maghreb," *LM*, Oct. 3, 2001. p. 9.

[74] "Chirac's attack on Congress has a bigger target," *IHT*, Nov. 9, 1999, p. 2.

[75] "*French and German publics' trust in the U.S. falls to new lows*," Office of Intelligence and Research, U.S. State Department, June 4, 2004, p. 1-2.

[76] Hans Blix, *Disarming Iraq, New York*: Pantheon Books, 2004, p. 156-157, 260-264; Report on "*The Future of Transatlantic Security: New Challenges*," French American Foundation conference of U.S., French, British, and German officials, Dec. 2002.

In: France in Focus
Editor: J.B. Lynch, pp. 51-70

ISBN 1-59454-935-4
© 2006 Nova Science Publishers, Inc.

Chapter 3

U.S.-FRENCH COMMERCIAL TIES [*]

Raymond J. Ahearn

SUMMARY

U.S. commercial ties with France are extensive, mutually profitable, and growing. With approximately $1 billion in commercial transactions taking place between the two countries *every business day* of the year, each country has an increasingly large stake in the health and openness of the other's economy.

France is the 9th largest merchandise trading partner for the United States and the United States is France's largest trading partner outside the European Union. In 2003, 64% or $29.7 billion of bilateral trade occurred in major industries such as aerospace, pharmaceuticals, medical and scientific equipment, electrical machinery, and plastics where both countries export and import similar products.

The United States and France also have a large and growing trade in services such as tourism, education, finance, insurance and other professional services. In 2002, France was the sixth largest market for U.S. exports of services and the seventh largest provider of services to the United States.

While trade in goods and services receives most of the attention in terms of the commercial relationship, foreign direct investment and the activities of foreign affiliates can be viewed as the backbone of the

---

[*] Excerpted from CRS Report RL32459, dated July 7, 2004.

commercial relationship. The scale of sales of U.S.-owned companies operating in France and French-owned companies operating in the United States outweighs trade transactions by a factor of *six* to *five*.

In 2002 France was the sixth largest host country for U.S. foreign direct investment abroad and the United States with investments valued at $43.9 billion was the number one foreign investor in France. During that same year, French companies had direct investments in the United States totaling $171 billion (historical cost basis), making France the second largest investor in the United States. French-owned companies employed some 578,600 workers in the United States in 2001 compared to 540,000 employees of U.S. companies invested in France.

Most U.S. trade and investment transactions with France, dominated by multinational companies, are non-controversial. Nevertheless, three prominent issues — agriculture, government intervention in corporate activity, and the war in Iraq —have contributed to increased bilateral tensions in recent years. The most pointed perhaps arose in early 2003 with reports of U.S. consumer boycotts of French goods and calls from some Members of Congress for trade retaliation against France (and Germany) due to foreign policy differences over the Iraq War.

The foreign policy dispute, however, appears *not* to have had much impact on sales of products such as French wines, perfumes and toiletries, travel goods and handbags, and cheeses that are most prone to being boycotted. While some public opinion polls suggest support for economic boycotts as a way of expressing opposition to France's position on Iraq, a substantial economic backlash appears unlikely due to the high degree of economic integration. Effective boycotts would jeopardize thousands of jobs on both sides of the Atlantic. This report will not be updated.

This report was written at the request of the co-chairs of the Congressional French Caucus.

OVERVIEW

U.S. commercial ties with France are extensive, mutually profitable, and growing. Each country has an increasingly large stake in the health and openness of the other's economy. While the relationship dates back to the colonial period, it is also constantly evolving.

The U.S. and French economies share many similarities. Based on a gross domestic product (GDP) of over $11 trillion, the United States is the world's largest economy. France with a GDP approaching $2 trillion is the world's sixth largest economy. France's population of 60 million has a per capita income (based on purchasing power parities in 2002) of $26,000 while the comparable figure for the United States, based on a population of 275 million, is $36,300.[1] As industrialized economies, both share similar structural attributes where over 70% of the civilian workforce is employed in services and less than 3% in agriculture.[2]

At the same time, the state still plays a larger role in the economy of France than in the United States. This is particularly true in the provision of services such as education and health care, but also in energy, telecommunications, and transport where state-owned companies play a prominent role. Policies geared to supporting national champions in leading sectors, to sustaining a network of personal relationships linking the heads of large companies with senior civil servants, and to rejecting American-style *laissez-faire* capitalism also distinguishes France from the United States.[3] Yet, prompted by mandates from the European Union, the government of France has acted to liberalize the vast majority of product markets, including energy, in recent years.[4]

Trade Ties

Differences in the role the state plays in the economy, however, have not precluded a growing number and type of international economic transactions from making the two economies increasingly interdependent. In the case of merchandise trade, France is the 9th largest trading partner for the United States and the United States is France's largest trading partner outside the European Union. As shown in **Table 1**, total trade turnover (exports plus imports) totaled $46 billion in 2003, with the United States running a $12.2 billion deficit.

Table 1. U.S. Trade with France in Goods, 1995-2003
(Billions of Dollars)

	1995	1996	1997	1998	1999	2000	2001	2002	2003
Exports	14.2	15.5	16.0	17.7	18.9	20.4	19.9	19.0	17.0
Imports	17.2	18.6	20.6	24.0	25.7	29.8	30.4	28.2	29.2
Balance	-3.0	-4.1	-4.6	-6.3	-6.8	-9.4	-10.5	-9.2	-12.2

Source: U.S. Census Bureau.

Most striking about U.S.-French merchandise trade is the extent to which it is concentrated in similar industries and sectors (so-called *intra-*

industry trade). In 2003, 64% or $29.7 billion of bilateral trade occurred in major industries such as aerospace, pharmaceuticals, medical and scientific equipment, electrical machinery, and plastics where both countries export and import similar products (see Tables C and D in the Appendix). Many of these products are components or capital goods used in the production of finished goods in both the United States and France. Furthermore, due to large amounts of foreign direct investment across both sides of the Atlantic, much of this *intra-industry* trade takes place as trade between parent companies and their affiliates (so-called *intra-firm* trade). This kind of trade, where large multinational companies, such as Michelin and General Electric, trade among their affiliates, accounted for $18 billion or 36% of total trade turnover in 2001.[5]

The overwhelming role that both *intra-industry* and *intra-firm* trade play in merchandise trade tends to limit targets of any potential trade retaliation. This is because restrictions placed on most of these traded items would adversely affect domestic production as well as employment of the country imposing the restriction.

The United States and France also have a large and growing trade in services such as tourism, education, finance, insurance, and other professional services. As shown in Table 2 , the U.S. exported $10.7 billion in services to France in 2002 and imported $9.6 billion in services. These amounts made France the sixth largest market for U.S. exports of services and the seventh largest provider of services to the United States.

Table 2 . U.S. Trade with France in Services, 1995-2002 (Billions of Dollars)

	1995	1996	1997	1998	1999	2000	2001	2002
Exports	7.9	8.9	9.3	9.6	10.0	10.5	10.1	10.7
Imports	5.9	6.0	6.6	7.4	8.0	10.5	9.9	9.6
Balance	2.0	2.9	2.7	2.2	2.0	0	0.2	1.1

Source: U.S. Bureau of Economic Analysis.

From 1995-1999, the United States experienced surpluses in services trade with France that averaged over $2 billion annually. While services trade was basically balanced in 2000 and 2001, the U.S. ran a $1.1 billion surplus in 2002 (the last year for which these data are available). As a result of services trade surpluses, the U.S. incurs smaller deficits with France, as shown in Table 3, on trade in both goods and services.

Table 3. U.S. Trade Balance with France on
Goods and Services, 1995-2002
(Billions of Dollars)

	1995	1996	1997	1998	1999	2000	2001	2002
Balance	1.0	-1.2	-1.9	-4.1	-4.8	-9.4	-10.3	-8.1

Source: U.S. Bureau of Economic Analysis.

Investment Ties

While trade in goods and services receives most of the attention in terms of U.S.-France commercial ties, foreign direct investment and the activities of foreign affiliates can be viewed as the backbone of the commercial relationship. Compared to trade flows, the scale of commercial activities of U.S.-owned companies operating in France and French-owned companies operating in the United States outweighs trade flows by a factor of *six* to *five*.

This key dynamic of the commercial relationship is illustrated in Table 4. In 2001, French companies sold $212 billion of goods and services to U.S. consumers while U.S. companies sold $148 billion of goods and services to French consumers. Of this combined $360 billion in sales, only $70 billion or 20% was accounted for by international trade (exports of goods and services from French companies to the U.S. and from U.S. companies to France). The vast majority (80%) was due to sales by U.S. foreign affiliates producing and selling in France and French foreign affiliates producing and selling in the United States. The combined U.S.-French annual $360 billion sales figure translates into over $1 billion in commercial transactions taking place *every business day* of the year.

Table 4. U.S. - France Commercial Interactions, 2001
(Billions of Dollars)

Commercial transaction	France	U.S.	Totals
Exports of goods	30.4	19.9	50.3
Exports of services	9.9	10.1	20.0
Foreign affiliate sales	172	117.8	289.8
Totals	212.3	147.8	360.1

Source: Bureau of Economic Analysis, Census Bureau.

In the case of foreign direct investment, France in 2002 was the sixth largest host country for overall U.S. foreign direct investment and the United

States was the number one foreign investor with investments valued at $43.9 billion (historical cost basis). During the same year, French companies had direct investments in the United States totaling $171 billion (valued on a historical cost basis), making France the second largest foreign investor in the United States in stock terms. Manufacturing accounted for 41% of total French investments and 47% of total U.S. investments.[6]

The assets of some 2,918 French-owned companies operating in the United States (2001 data) totaled $535 billion, up nearly 700% from $77.5 billion in 1990. The 1,286 U.S.-owned companies operating in France had $191 billion in total assets in 2001, up from $78 billion in 1990 (see Tables H and I).

The total gross product or value added of French-owned companies operating in the United States in 2001 was $40 billion, up 200% from $19.2 billion in 1993 (the first year this data was collected).[7] This $40 billion gross product figure is greater than the total gross national product of countries such as Morocco, Ukraine, and Vietnam. At the same time, U.S. companies contributed $34.4 billion towards France's GDP in 2001, a sum exceeding the gross national products of Bolivia and Guatemala.[8]

Affiliate sales are the primary means by which French companies deliver goods and services to U.S. consumers. In 2001, French affiliate sales totaled $188 billion, up from $81.9 billion in 1990. Adjusting the $188 billion figure down by $16 billion — which was the value of French affiliate exports to the world in 2001 — translates into $172 billion in French affiliate sales to U.S. consumers, an amount that is 4.6 times greater than total French exports to the United States.

Sales of U.S. affiliates operating in France totaled $135 billion in 2001, up from $102 billion in 1990. Adjusting for possible double-counting by subtracting the $4.1 billion in exports shipped by U.S. affiliates to the United States gives a net sales figure of $130.9 billion. This figure, in turn, swamps the $19.9 billion in U.S. exports of goods to France by a factor of 6.5.

French-owned companies employed some 578,600 workers in the United States in 2001, up from 338,000 in 1990 but down from 655,000 in 2000. Of this total 262,000 were in manufacturing, 47,000 in wholesale trade, and 38,000 in retail trade. The largest 100 French companies such as Lafarge, Michelin, Sodexho (hotels and food service), EADS (European Aeronautic and Defense Company), Pernod-Richard, and Thomson account for 450,000 (or 78%) of the employment.[9]

A breakdown of employment by state indicates that the top 10 states hosting French subsidiaries are California (63,600), New York (51,000), Texas (50,600), Illinois (29,600), New Jersey (28,400), Pennsylvania

(26,800), Florida (25,800), Ohio (23,800), South Carolina (19,400) and Indiana (18,900).

U.S. companies invested in France had 540,500 employees in 2001, the vast majority French citizens. Of this total, 245,000 or 45% were employed in manufacturing industries such as chemicals (49,000), computers and electronic products (28,000), and machinery (25,000). An additional 64,000 people were employed in wholesale trade and 22,000 in scientific and technical services. Coca Cola, for example, has about 2,600 employees in 19 production sites in France.[10]

French companies are also active in doing research and development (RandD) in the United States. In 2001 they spent $3.2 billion on RandD, more than twice as much as the $1.4 billion that U.S. companies spent in France.[11] These expenditures can take a variety of forms. L'Oréal, a Paris-based cosmetics firm, for example, in 2003 set-up a research institute — L'Oréal Institute for Ethnic Hair and Skin Research —with an $1 million investment. This French-owned company reportedly plans to earmark 4% of its annual U.S. sales of $22 million for development of hair spray and skin creams dedicated to the African-American market.[12]

Through the MIT-France Program, the French government also plays a role in supporting research and development in the United States. Funded by matching $1 million contributions from France and MIT, the program was created in 2000 to support collaboration in science and technology between the two countries, including internships in France for MIT students. In the three years of the program, many of the 200 participating French scientists have taken on prominent positions at Boston-area biotech companies such as Eukarion, Biogen, and Genetix Pharmaceuticals. French scientists have also founded start-up companies in the United States such as Idenix Pharmaceuticals, which develops drugs for the treatment of viral and infectious diseases.[13]

Tensions and Disagreements

France, as a member of the European Union, adopts the same trade policy as other members of the EU.[14] By sharing common tariff and non-tariff policies with other EU members and by adopting EU-wide regulations and standards, there are few trade disputes that can be considered U.S.-French bilateral disagreements per se. Most U.S. trade and investment with France, dominated by multinational companies and intra-firm trade, is non-controversial Nevertheless, three prominent issues—agriculture, government intervention in corporate activity, and the war in Iraq —have contributed to increased bilateral tensions in recent years.

Agriculture

Agricultural trade disputes historically have been the major sticking point in U.S.-France commercial relations. Although the agricultural sector accounts for a declining percentage of output and employment in both countries, it has produced a disproportionate amount of trade tensions between the two sides.

From the U.S. perspective, the restrictive trade regime set up by the Common Agricultural Policy (CAP) has been the real villain. It has been a longstanding U.S. contention that the CAP is the largest single distortion of global agricultural trade. American farmers and policymakers have complained over the years that U.S. sales and profits are adversely affected by (1) EU restrictions on market access that have protected the European market for European farmers; by (2) EU export subsidies that have deflated U.S. sales to third markets; and by (3) EU domestic income support programs that have kept non-competitive European farmers in business.

France's agricultural sector, which in terms of output and land is the largest in Europe, has long been the biggest beneficiary of the CAP. In 2002, French farmers received 9.8 billion euros in CAP subsidies out of a total EU outlay of 43.2 billion euros.[15] Acting to continue benefits and subsidies for its farmers, the French position can determine the limits and parameters of the European Commission's negotiating flexibility on a range of agricultural issues that are of keen interest to the United States. The most prominent and perhaps important example relates to current efforts to get the WTO Doha round of multilateral trade negotiations back on track by reducing agricultural subsidies. While the European Commission on May 10, 2004 offered to eliminate $3.3 billion in export subsidies, François Loos, the French trade minister, balked on the grounds that the commission exceeded its mandate.[16] Other examples where the French position arguably has made settlement of disputes more difficult include expanded trademark protection for wines, cheeses, and other food products linked to specific regions, limits on research and use of genetically-modified (GM) crops, and a ban on the importation of beef treated with hormones.[17]

France tends to receive backing for its position opposing many proposed reforms of the CAP, as well as on other agricultural issues that adversely affect U.S. interests, from Italy, Spain, Greece and Portugal. Germany, which pays around 50% of the EU's $100 billion budget, tends to receive support for agricultural reforms from the Netherlands, Sweden, and the

United Kingdom, the other countries that are net financial contributors to the CAP. While the May 1, 2004 entry of 10 new countries into the EU should over time increase pressures for reform of the CAP, France is likely to insist that reductions of support levels be phased in over a long time period in order to allow French farmers plenty of time to adjust.

The U.S. and France have also recently been at loggerheads over food-safety issues. Last year and in early 2004 the EU suspended imports of live poultry and eggs from the United States after a case of highly contagious avian flu emerged in Texas. Then in February of this year the United States imposed an import ban on French cold cuts and foie gras because of sanitation concerns. While both bans (the EU ban has been suspended) may be due to legitimate health safety concerns, underlying suspicions that the bans are politically motivated are not far from the surface, thus highlighting ongoing tensions between the two sides.[18]

Despite the agricultural trade tensions, each side remains a relatively modest agricultural market for the other's products. U.S. agricultural exports to France, totaling some $600 million annually, consist primarily of bulk commodities such as soybeans and products, feeds, and fodders. French agricultural exports to the United States, which amount to more than $900 million annually, are mostly higher value-added products such as cheese and processed products, beverages, and spirits.[19]

Government Intervention in Corporate Activity

Despite significant reform and privatization over the past 15 years, the center-right French government continues to play a larger role in influencing corporate activity than does the U.S. government. This difference is manifested not only in the French government's continuing direct control of key companies, but also in its continuing proclivity to influence mergers involving French firms. The French government's close corporate ties have also embroiled it in embarrassing disclosures related to an on-going investigation of Credit Lyonnais's 12-year old acquisition of a California insurance company. Nevertheless, although bilateral disputes may be more prone to occur because of the French government's interventionist tendencies, the dictates of EU laws as well as the urgent need to raise the revenues that accompany privatization efforts, are weakening the French *dirigiste* tradition.

In 1997 the socialist government of France restarted a process of privatization and opening of government-controlled firms to private investment that had begun in the 1980s, and the program has been continued by the center-right government that took power in 2002. As a result, by 2003 there were fewer than a dozen public enterprises of any significant size still wholly owned by the state.[20] These included the leading electricity and gas suppliers (EDF and GDF), the quasi-monopoly supplier of postal services (La Poste), the national rail operator (SNCF), a defense equipment munitions manufacturer (GIAT Industries), and an aircraft manufacturer (Snecma). In addition, the state retains a controlling interest in a number of enterprises listed on the stock exchange. These include companies such as Air France, France Telecom, Renault, and Thales (a defense electronics company previously called Thomson CSF). The government also has more limited stakes in Bull, EADS, Dassault Systems and many other firms.[21]

On February 24, 2004, the French government announced its intention to sell a minority interest in Snecma, the aircraft manufacturer that supplied engines for the Rafale and Mirage military aircraft. This partial privatization could be significant since it will affect a company that is now 97% government-owned and deemed by the French government to be operating in a "strategic" sector. The aim, according to the Ministry of Finance, is to allow Snecma to deepen its longstanding partnership with General Electric. An expected $2-$3 billion in receipts could be allocated for capital infusion in other state-owned enterprises or to pay for the state-funded rescue of Credit Lyonnais, a bank that failed in the 1990s.[22]

Despite this example of a renewed government commitment to its privatization program, the French government continues to promote national champions as well. Over the past two years, for example, the government has acted to prevent publishing and utilities divisions of Vivendi Universal from falling into foreign hands and it has also organized state-sponsored "bail-outs" of France Telecom, Alstom, a big engineering company, and Bull, a computer manufacturer.[23]

The most recent example of French government intervention in the marketplace centered on the creation of a national pharmaceuticals champion. It did this in April 2004 by publically backing the merger of Sanofi-Synthelabo, a Paris-based pharmaceuticals company, with Aventis, a French-German competitor. The merger will make Sanofi-Aventis the world's third largest drug company, behind a U.S. company, Pfizer, and a U.K. company, GlaxoSmithKline. By opposing a rival bid and approach by the Swiss-based Novartis Group, the French government, according to critics, reinforced the belief that it plays a big role in all economic decisions in the French market. Prime Minister Jean-Pierre Raffarin countered that "this does not mean France will be nationalistic, individualistic and egotistical, but will be open to projects with our European and other partners."[24] Nevertheless, the message that the current government, like many of its predecessors, intends to play an active role in the economy that on occasion may favor national control of business may not be lost on foreign investors.[25]

The French government's longstanding propensity to intervene in the marketplace also is related, in part, to the on-going scandal and litigation involving the French bank Credit Lyonnais. In the early 1990s, Credit Lyonnais, then a huge state-owned bank, violated certain U.S. laws in an effort to purchase Executive Life, a failed California-based insurance company. In January of 2004, the French government was forced to plead guilty in U.S. District Court in California to fraud and French taxpayers had to pay $375 million of the $770 million criminal case fines. In a larger civil lawsuit that is scheduled for trial in February 2005, California's insurance regulator is seeking up to $5 billion in damages.[26]

Iraq War

In the era of the Cold War, there was considerable concern that trade disputes between allies could undermine political and security ties. Deep differences over the Iraq war between the United States and many of its allies, particularly France and Germany, reversed this Cold War concern into whether foreign policy disputes can weaken or undermine strong commercial ties.

Specific concerns that divisions over Iraq could spill over into the trade arena arose in early 2003 with reports of U.S. consumer boycotts of French goods and calls from some U.S. lawmakers for trade retaliation against France (and Germany). The spike in bilateral tensions and hard feelings, however, appears *not* to have had much impact on sales of the products most likely prone to being boycotted. These include French wines, perfumes and toiletries, travel goods and handbags, and cheeses.[27]

As shown in **Table 5**, U.S. imports of these four categories of French products all increased in absolute terms and as a share of total U.S. imports from France. While total U.S. imports from France increased by 3.5% in 2002/2003, U.S. imports of wine increased by 21.5%, imports of perfumes and toiletries by 17.8%, imports of travel goods and handbags by 31.3%, and imports of cheese and curd by 20.0%. All four categories also increased their share of total imports.[28]

Table 5. U.S. Imports from France of Selected Products, 2001-2003

HS #	Description	(Millions of U.S. Dollars)			% Share of Total Imports from France			% Change
		2001	2002	2003	2001	2002	2003	2003/2002
2204	Wines of fresh grapes	826	933	1,133	2.7	3.3	3.9	21.5
3303	Perfumes and toiletries	511	609	717	1.9	2.2	2.5	17.8
4204	Travel goods; handbags	147	159	209	0.5	0.6	0.7	31.3
0406	Cheese and curd	72	90	108	0.2	0.3	0.4	20.0

Source: World Trade Atlas.

The trade data are somewhat surprising given some of the public opinion polling that was done in the spring of 2003. One survey of 1,000 adult Americans, for example, attempted to gauge consumer sentiments towards substituting U.S. or other products for French products as a way of expressing opposition to the France's position on Iraq. Of those polled, 15% indicated they would likely participate in a boycott. And a high percentage of this group tended to be white, middle-to-upper income, more highly educated, and conservative — a profile similar to that of high- income luxury brand buyers of such well recognized French products as Perrier, Evian, Beaujolais, and Lancôme.[29]

In France and Germany, one poll found that two-thirds of college graduates with annual incomes larger than $75,000 surveyed in December 2003 and January 2004, said that they are less likely to buy U.S. products because of the Bush Administration. Yet many U.S. companies such as Ford, Kodak, and McDonald's say there has been no effect on sales as of May 2004.[30]

While there are few signs that goods and services clearly identified with France or the United States are being boycotted, consumer sentiments as expressed in these polls could be warnings of the potential fallout from foreign policy disputes. Nevertheless, a substantial economic backlash appears unlikely due to the high degree of economic integration. Effective boycotts would jeopardize thousands of jobs on both sides of the Atlantic.

APPENDIX: TRADE AND FOREIGN INVESTMENT DATA

Table A. Top Ten U.S. Trading Partners, 2003
(billions of U.S. dollars)

Country	Trade Turnover (exports and imports)
Canada	394
Mexico	236
China	181
Japan	170
Germany	97
United Kingdom	77
Korea, Republic of	61
Taiwan	49
France	46
Italy	36

Source: U.S. Census Bureau.

Table B. France's Top Trading Partners, 2002
(billions of dollars)

Country	Trade Turnover (exports plus imports)
Germany	113.3
Italy	58.6
United Kingdom	56.6
Belgium	52.9
Spain	51.9
United States	48.3

Source: IMF Directions of Trade.

Table C. Major U.S. Exports to France, 2003
(billions of dollars)

Rank	Harmonized System 2-Digit Description	Value
1	84-Nuclear reactors, boilers, machinery and mechanical appliances such as gas turbines, computers, and office machinery	4.9
2	90-Optical, photographic, and medical instruments	2.0
3	85-Electrical machinery and equipment, such as integrated circuits	1.6
4	88-Aircraft, spacecraft, and parts thereof	1.5
5	29-Organic chemicals, such as hormones and glycosides	1.3
6	30-Pharmaceutical products	1.1
7	38-Miscellaneous chemical products such as laboratory reagents	0.5
8	87-Vehicles and parts	0.4
9	39-Plastics and articles thereof	0.4
10	37-Photographic or cinematographic goods such as photographic film	0.3

Source: U.S. International Trade Commission.

Table D. Major U.S. Imports from France, 2003
(billions of dollars)

Rank	Harmonized System 2-Digit Description	Value
1	84-Nuclear reactors, boilers, machinery and mechanical appliances such as gas turbines, bulldozers, and machinery for working rubber or plastics	4.3
2	88-Aircraft, spacecraft, and parts thereof	4.2
3	30-Pharmaceutical products	2.5
4	22-Beverages, and spirits such as wine and liqueurs	2.1
5	85-Electrical machinery and equipment such as electronic integrated circuits, T.V. equipment and video cameras	2.1
6	29-Organic chemicals such as heterocyclic compounds	1.5
7	97-Works of art, collectors' pieces and antiques	1.4
8	87-Vehicles and parts	1.2
9	90-Optical, photographic, medical or surgical instruments	1.1
10	33-Essential oils, perfumes, and cosmetic preparations	1.1

Source: U.S. International Trade Commission.

Table E. U.S. Total Exports to France by Top 25 States
(millions of dollars)

Rank	State	2001	2002	2003
	All States	19,895	19,018	17,068
1	California	2,241	1,885	1,915
2	New York	1,481	1,317	1,261
3	Connecticut	1,416	1,178	1,095
4	Indiana	669	638	922
5	Texas	1,013	929	905
6	Puerto Rico	615	751	779
7	Ohio	1,448	1,068	768
8	Kentucky	432	795	740
9	Washington	1,252	1,953	684
10	Illinois	709	623	679
11	Massachusetts	865	922	619
12	New Jersey	658	622	602
13	Florida	399	388	397
14	Michigan	371	335	380
15	Pennsylvania	440	369	372
16	Wisconsin	366	341	371
17	North Carolina	348	252	360
18	Georgia	343	338	358
19	Arizona	632	442	350
20	Minnesota	335	353	328
21	South Carolina	261	320	274
22	Colorado	340	282	267
23	Alabama	317	230	221
24	Tennessee	279	241	221
25	Iowa	157	197	204

Source: U.S. Census Bureau.

Table F. Foreign Direct Investment in the
United States: Top Five Countries
(billions of dollars)

Direct Investment Position on a Historical Cost Basis					
	1998	1999	2000	2001	2002
United Kingdom	137	154	278	269	283
France	60	90	126	148	171
Germany	93	112	122	164	137
Japan	134	154	160	150	152
Netherlands	92	125	139	158	155

Source: Survey of Current Business.

Table G. Employment of French Nonbank U.S. Affiliates,
by Top 15 States, 2001

	Total Employment 578,600	
Rank	State	
1	California	63,600
2	New York	51,000
3	Texas	50,600
4	Illinois	29,600
5	New Jersey	28,400
6	Pennsylvania	26,800
7	Florida	25,800
8	Ohio	23,800
9	South Carolina	19,400
10	Indiana	18,900
11	Massachusetts	18,100
12	North Carolina	16,700
13	Georgia	15,700
14	Michigan	14,100
15	Virginia	14,000

Source: Bureau of Economic Analysis.

Table H. French Foreign Direct Investment
in the United States, 1990-2001

Year	No. of French-owned Companies	No. of Employees	Assets (billions $)	Sales (billions $)	Gross Product (billions $)
1990	1,759	338,000	176	82	N/A
1991	1,893	364,900	162	89	N/A
1992	2,327	363,400	273	102	N/A
1993	1,862	359,400	214	97	19
1994	2,124	376,200	211	112	23
1995	2,406	346,000	232	111	24
1996	2,521	420,200	283	132	34
1997	2,239	415,000	328	136	36
1998	2,250	527,500	390	142	37
1999	2,686	614,300	523	170	45
2000	2,986	654,800	484	195	55
2001	2,918	578,600	535	188	40

Source: U.S. Department of Commerce, Bureau of Economic Analysis.

Table I. U.S. Foreign Direct Investment in France, 1990-2001

Year	No. of U.S.-owned Companies	No. of Employees	Assets (billions $)	Sales (billions $)
1990	1,026	419,700	78	102
1991	1,052	439,300	83	103
1992	1,067	404,800	89	104
1993	1,072	400,300	82	99
1994	1,262	397,800	133	107
1995	1,228	416,000	141	125
1996	1,270	448,800	146	136
1997	1,299	464,400	150	130
1998	1,260	492,300	168	139
1999	1,269	575,300	205	144
2000	1,256	589,300	187	138
2001	1,286	578,300	191	135

Source: U.S. Department of Commerce, Bureau of Economic Analysis.

REFERENCES

[1]   *CIA World Factbook*, 2003.

[2]   OECD data.

[3]   The contrast in unemployment rates, with France approaching 10% and the United States under 6%, is another major difference between the two economies.

[4]   The Economist Intelligence Unit, France: Country Profile 2004, pp. 32-33. Available at [*http://www.eiu.com/schedule*].

[5]   CRS calculation based on Department of Commerce, Bureau of Economic Analysis data.

[6]   Unless otherwise noted, all foreign direct investment data come from the U.S. Department of Commerce, Bureau of Economic Analysis.

[7]   Gross product is defined as the market value of goods and services produced by labor and property located in the United States. Gross product can be measured as gross output (sales or receipts and other operating income plus inventory change) minus intermediate inputs (purchased goods and services).

[8]   GDP data from *World Bank Development Report*, 2003.

[9]   Embassy of France. "Economic Relations between France and the United States," January 2004. Available at [*http://www.onfo-france-usa.org*].

[10]   *French News Digest*, "U.S. Coca-Cola to Launch Mineral Water in France April 2004," January 29, 2004.

[11]   Data from U.S. Bureau of Economic Analysis.

[12]   Brieger, Peter. "L'Oréal looks to needs of U.S. minority buyers: The French cosmetics firm opened a research institute dedicated to developing products for the African-American consumer," *Financial Post,* April 19, 2004.

[13]   Denison, D.C. "French Seek to Mend Rift Over Iraq with Science." *Boston Globe*, April 28, 2003.

[14]   For discussion of U.S.-EU commercial ties, see CRS Report RL30608, *EU-U.S. Economic Ties: Framework, Scope, and Magnitude*, by William Cooper.

[15]   European Commission, Directorate for Agriculture, Financial Report 2002. Found at [*http://europa.eu.int/comm/agriculture/agrista/2003/table_en/342.pdf*].

[16]   Meller, Paul. "France Splits With Europe Over Farm Subsidy Plan," *NYT*, May 11, 2004, p. W1. Some observers argue that French

opposition to reform is often tactical and that it has not prevented substantial reform of the CAP.

[17] Trademark protection for geographic indications is also an issue of great importance for Italy (parma ham and parmesan cheese), Greece (feta cheese), Hungary (tokay wine), and Portugal (porto wine). Denmark, Italy, and Germany are other EU countries taking the lead on limits on research and use of GM crops and most all EU members strongly support the ban on the importation of beef treated with hormones. For further discussion of these disputes, see CRS Report RS21569, *Geographical Indications and WTO Negotiations*, by Charles Hanrahan, CRS ebtra53, *Biotechnology and Agricultural Trade*, by Geoffrey Becker and Charles Hanrahan, and CRS Report RL31841, *Agricultural Trade Issues in the 108th Congress*, by Geoffrey Becker and Charles Hanrahan.

[18] Dupont, Veronique. "As Feathers Fly Between U.S. and France, A Desperate Hunt for Foie Gras," *Agence France Presse*, February 25, 2004.

[19] U.S. Department of State, *"Background Note: France,"* February 2004, p.5.

[20] EIU, *Country Profile 2004*. p. 32.

[21] *Ibid.*

[22] *EIU Country Report, April* 2004, p. 19.

[23] *Ibid.*

[24] Johnson, Jo, "Deal is a setback to investment," *FT*, April 27, 2004, p. 18.

[25] France's newly appointed Finance Minister, Nicolas Sarkozy, in his first news conference, called for relaxation of EU state-aid rules to allow national governments to expend public funds on enhancing the competitiveness of key companies. See Bennhold, Katrin, " Sakozy Urges Europe to Forge Industrial Hubs," *International Herald Tribune (IHT)*, May 5, 2004, p.1.

[26] Carreyrou, John and Glenn R. Simpson, "Foreign Policy: How Insurance Spat Further Frayed U.S.-French Ties — Paris Forks Over $375 Million in Executive Life Dispute; Gucci Owner Pinned Down — California's Civil Suit Looms," *The Wall Street Journal*, April 16, 2004.

[27] This is an illustrative, not exhaustive, list of products that are likely to be targets of boycotts because they have a strong element of brand identification with France, and tend to be luxury items.

[28] In January-February 2004, total U.S. imports from France were down
1.76% over January-February 2003, but three of the four categories
experienced healthy growth with perfumes up 13.1%, travel goods up
5.5%, and cheese and curd up 25.5%. Wine imports, however, were
down 4.7% over the January/February 2003 level.

[29] "American Consumers Split Over Substitutions and Boycotts of
French," Washington, D.C. April 21, 2003. Fleischman-Hillard
International Communications. [http://www.fleishman.com/news/pro
41703.html].

[30] Romero, Simon. "War and Abuse Do Little Harm To U.S. Brands,"
NYT, May 9, 2004, p. A1.

INDEX

T